Donatus Bibliothecae

THIS BOOK GIVEN TO
FORT WORTH PUBLIC LIBRARY
IN HONOR OF

William J. Thornton, Jr.

GUEST SPEAKER
ROTARY CLUB OF FORT WORTH

September 4, 1998

Winning 'em Over

A New Model for Managing in the Age of Persuasion

Jay A. Conger

Simon & Schuster

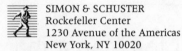

SIMON & SCHUSTER
Rockefeller Center
1230 Avenue of the Americas
New York, NY 10020

10   9   8   7   6   5   4   3   2   1

Library of Congress Cataloging-in-Publication Data

Conger, Jay Alden.
    Winning 'em over : a new model for managing
in the age of persuasion / by Jay A. Conger.
        p.   cm.
    Includes bibliographical references and index.
    1. Persuasion (Psychology).   2. Teams in the
workplace—Management.   3. Management.
I. Title.
HD66.C565   1998
658.4'052—dc21   98-9632   CIP
ISBN 0-684-80772-6

To Nadège, the love of my life

Acknowledgments

A book is never the product of a single individual. Though my name appears on the cover, I owe a number of people a great debt for helping me along the rocky and wondrous path of writing a book.

First and foremost, I want to acknowledge Tom Congdon who is a remarkably talented editor. One of the challenges facing academics who wish to write for a broader audience is our love of technical jargon and complicated thoughts. We produce cluttered gardens. Tom's artistry recrafted my garden of thoughts. He simplified my arrangements into eye-pleasing designs, pruned my unruly collection of plants into lovely hedges, and added more palettes of appealing colors. In the process, he has taught me how to become a far more effective writer. I am grateful for his talent.

A friend of mine, Jim Moore, knew that I was writing this book. Jim had just finished his own book and had done an extensive—and I mean extensive—search for a talented agent. He said to me, "I have found the best agent in the business—Richard Pine." He then rattled off a list of Pine's clients, which sounded like a "Who's Who" list of authors. Despite feeling a bit intimidated, I was introduced to Richard by Jim. To my surprise and delight, Richard immediately saw the potential in this book. He sensed that I was chronicling a revolution in management. He was certain that managers would find its ideas and techniques compelling. The next thing I knew Richard was off promoting my book. Since then, he has been a terrific guide in the complex and challenging world of book publishing.

I have also had some wonderful reviewers along the way, individuals who helped me to clarify and refine my thoughts, who made the text more useful and more engaging. I am especially indebted to Brian Levitt and Mark Burnett who were extremely helpful with their insights. Brian is CEO of Imasco, a diversified, multibillion-dollar company. He is a wonderfully bright and thoughtful person who loves the art of persuasion, having been a lawyer in his former life. He provided me with a critical perspective from the senior-most levels of a corporation. Mark, on the other hand, is a very sharp Generation Xer who has been a friend for some time. He made sure that the text made sense to the newest generation of managers. I am also thankful to Phil and Carol Champagne, Karen Fries of Microsoft, and Monica Ruffo of Cossette Communications. They took the time and energy to delve into early versions of this book and provide detailed comments on how to enhance my ideas.

Karen Fries and Monica Ruffo along with Jim Dawson of Zebco, Orit Gadiesh of Bain, David Marcello of Chrysler, and Zig Ziegler gave generously of their time to be case studies for this project. As well, several others who appear as disguised characters made similar investments.

Some time after I had signed on with Simon & Schuster, Richard Pine informed me that my editor would be Dominick Anfuso. Dominick, he said, was one of the company's top editors. Just as my friend Jim had done, Richard then listed some of the remarkable books for which Dominick has been responsible. Suddenly, I had two talented figures in the publishing world behind my manuscript. It was a wonderful turn of events. Dominick, like Richard, has since played an instrumental role in helping me to realize this book's fullest potential.

Deletha Gafford, at the University of Southern California, and Pina Vicario, at McGill University, have provided wonderful secretarial support. They transformed my scribblings into neatly ordered words and marvelously aligned paragraphs. They persevered in the face of faulty software and the challenges of writing via the Internet. A book is a mammoth undertaking not only for its author but for those who put its words to type. Deletha and Pina deserve a special thanks.

Finally, my wife, Nadège, has been both a reviewer and soul-mate for this journey. She has shared with me in the highs and lows of writing and has helped me immeasurably to persevere in the seemingly never-ending challenges of writing a book. She has also always been nearby with a bottle of good French champagne to celebrate the victories.

Jay A. Conger
Los Angeles, California

Contents

Introduction

This book chronicles a revolution. It is about a revolution in how we manage others. You and I are in the midst of witnessing an ancient model of managing built around commands and hierarchy give way to one built around persuasion and teamwork.

The central idea that I wish to convey is that we live in a remarkably less homogeneous and traditional workplace than what existed just two decades ago. It is one built upon different generations, different attitudes, different power bases. It is also built around new technologies, flatter hierarchies, and people working in groups of peers. All of these forces are producing this revolution.

Until recently, managers could simply influence others by the power of their position and the right to command that accompanied that position. Bosses had what we call formal authority. It ensured respect and obedience from those beneath to get many things done: the John Wayne school of management. There you are, high in the saddle. So you mosey into town, bark out some orders, watch everybody scatter to get the job done, and then you ride on to the next problem situation—mission accomplished.

Today the power of this school of managing is diminishing. Instead, new generations of managers and subordinates are re-shaping what it means to be "the boss." They are a sharp contrast with previous command-style generations. For example, today's most effective bosses are influencing others to action through novel and positive forms of persuasion. As a result, the best among this new generation of managers can get levels of commitment and motivation that their predecessors could only dream of.

The challenge that this revolution presents, however, is that it is a gradual one. It has been sneaking up on us so its changes are less immediately apparent. Some might call it a quiet revolution. As a result, we are a bit like fish in an aquarium. The fish have a very difficult time feeling the water that surrounds them—much like the air for humans. A very gradual change in the water's temperature at first goes unnoticed. But at a certain point as it increases, it invisibly begins to affect how those fish will act. The changes that I am about to describe in the world of management are similar to this analogy. Though they began incrementally, they have reached the magnitude where they are today, radically re-shaping how we lead and manage our colleagues at work. The dilemma is that we are only partially aware of their impact. As a result, just a few of us have fully realized that a new style of managing and leading is in order. The rest of us sense that some-thing big is afoot, but the shape of the new skills we need is not yet completely apparent. I am going to change all of that for you. I am going to fast-forward you to becoming an exceptional boss in this new era of management.

What You Will Learn

One important aim of this book is to challenge your stereotypes of persuasion. We usually think of persuasion as something reserved for salespeople—certainly not for managers. What I am going to propose to you is that, quite to the contrary, persuasion skills have become absolutely essential to the job of managing—far more than we might imagine. Much of what a good manager does today is sell: sell their ideas to coworkers; sell their organizations on change; sell their bosses on new investments. But it's not tradi-tional selling. A large part of what we do as effective managers is to find optimal solutions for problems through investigation, discussion, and debate. We then convince our organization to get behind them. It is in the convincing part that we face our greatest hurdles—getting buy-in. This is where the skills of constructive persuasion play a vital role. So leave behind your older notions of persuasion. It's time for a paradigm shift. Your effectiveness depends on it.

Why constructive persuasion has become so important to daily managing is due to three fundamental forces: *(1)* new generations of managers and executives, *(2)* the popularity of the cross-functional team, and *(3)* computer technologies. Each of these forces is radically undermining the traditional sources of a manager's power. As a result, managers need new understandings, new tools, new ways to influence others. Most of all they need the ability to persuade and convince rather than command and direct. Success at these skills will not only get you greater commitment to initiatives but, just as important, better ideas and solutions from your staff and colleagues, and much better teamwork.

You'll feel a difference in yourself, too. You'll be surprised at how much more effective you are with peers and bosses. You'll also find yourself getting deeper buy-in to ideas and initiatives. Your confidence will improve. You'll start to understand why getting commitment to your suggestions in the past has often been a long, painful slog. You'll learn that it doesn't have to be that way. With a bit of effective detective work, you'll learn how to create solutions where you and others win together. Finally, you'll find yourself becoming a lot wiser about people and about leading others.

The goal of this book then is to provide you with the latest tools so that you can accomplish these outcomes and in turn navigate more easily in this new world of managing. If you imagine yesterday's generations of managers using hammers and nails to manage, today's tools are far more dynamic and sophisticated. They are the equivalent of a multimedia, interactive personal computer. This book is essentially a tool box filled with these new, powerful skills. I have illustrated each skill with rich examples from actual case studies and with lots of insider information on how you can turn a particular technique into actions. I have also organized these techniques of persuasion management into a straightforward framework that shows you how to integrate one technique into another. In addition, there are exercises to help you quickly hone the new skills that you will be learning.

At the back of the book are three appendices that contain all the information you'll need to understand why the world of management is changing. These describe how the world has been and what it is becoming. To be truly effective at any new management practice, we need to understand how it fits with the demands of our current environment. So I will show you in some detail the fundamental changes that are promoting the new style of managing—the new boss. In a nutshell, we are leaving one age—the age of command—and moving into a new one—the age of persuasion. The appendices give you vital background information on these profound changes.

Constructive Persuasion

The other day I was in the locker room of my gym. A stranger turned to me and said, "You look like a million dollars." I was quite surprised. Naturally, I imagined for a moment looking like a million dollars. But I had a small, uncomfortable feeling. After all, I know that I am not Tom Cruise. Suspicious, I smiled and then looked for a clue as to what he might be wanting. There on his gym bag was the sign I was looking for. It said "Mitchum Investments." He was, of course, thinking "Here's a potential investor—flatter him and his money will be mine!" Needless to say, I immediately discounted the compliment. I was not persuaded. I use this example to illustrate the absolute opposite of what this book is all about. If you want to learn about how to manipulate others into things you alone want, then this volume will not be for you. It is not a manual for the self-serving.

This book is instead about a practical form of *positive* persuasion, persuasion employed in the service of helping people to be better leaders and managers. It is about improving organizational performance rather than enriching a single individual. It is a manual for managers who want to become far more effective in a world where workplace relationships are extremely challenging. It is a manual for managers who have realized that their own formal authority is not enough to mobilize their organizations.

The story of the origins of this book perhaps best captures what you will learn about this new and important "take" on persuasion. I began with the notion of writing a book on leadership in teams. But the first research interview changed my course. I was meeting with team leaders of engineering projects in an aerospace company. As I was interviewing, I began to realize that the absolute best performing leader of all the teams was a young engineer who *(1)* was deeply concerned for the well-being of his team, *(2)* wanted the best possible outcome for everyone and the organization, and *(3)* was a master at what I call constructive persuasion. In interviews at other companies, I began to see this same pattern of constructive persuasion over and over again among my top-performing team leaders. I knew then that I was on to something. I started to realize that not only were teams the crucial testing grounds for constructive persuasion but that the newer generations of executives and managers were hothouses for such innovative ways of managing. These generations had different expectations about authority than their predecessors. They preferred to be *convinced* into action rather than ordered. They were more naturally drawn to bosses who managed through constructive persuasion. Simultaneously, I had also been involved in studying leaders orchestrating large-scale change in their organizations. The best of these change-agent leaders were using remarkably similar approaches to persuasion. These discoveries led to the book as it now stands.

My mission then became one of searching out the "best in class," such as my young engineer. I would learn from the most outstanding. As a result, I have spent the last several years studying managers who are very good at the new skills of constructive persuasion. I have distilled what these exceptional managers do so that you and I might become just as effective as they are. In the process, I have also learned that just about anyone can transform himself* with practice into this new breed. Age, gender, and industry background are no barriers. You too can become a master of constructive persuasion. You too can become an exceptional boss in the age of persuasion. The tools await you in the chapters to come.

---

* When the pronoun "he" ("himself") is used to mean "person" throughout this book, the reader is asked to read it as "he (himself) or she (herself)." To use "he or she" in every instance would be awkward and distracting, and at the moment there seems to be no workable alternative to the singular pronoun. In time, a preferable designation will doubtless evolve in the ever-vigorous English language.

1
Welcome to
the Future

Let's begin with the parable of Jacobson and Keene. Mike Jacobson was known in the company as a real comer. He'd quickly risen up the ranks to senior management and at forty-five was in line for a vice presidency. In what was clearly a prelude to that promotion, Mike had been put in charge of the company's new-product development team.

It was a crucial assignment. The team was created in response to competition from companies who now were able to introduce three times as many new products as Mike's firm could. Over the last two years, these rivals had been like sharks, chewing off some 4.5 percent of the company's market share. The team's meetings, unfortunately, had not been going well. And today was no different.

The big issue before the meeting was how to design the next generation of the company's Personal Digital Assistant (PDA), a small, handheld computer that could take notes, send faxes, and receive e-mail. If the new model succeeded in the marketplace, it could reverse the company's downward slide. The question was, how fancy should it be?

Mike was from marketing, and he'd been arguing that to attract customers the PDA should have lots of new features. But no one had seemed to be listening. The team's attention was fastened upon Peter Keene, the recently appointed manager of production. Peter was emphasizing low price and snafu-free production; he believed the product should be simple and stripped down, with fewer features. To Mike's dismay Peter seemed to be not just winning the debate but emerging as the team's real leader. He wasn't doing it on purpose; it was just happening.

"The guy is some kind of genius," Mike thought to himself. Peter had this uncanny ability to get his point across.

Mike glanced at his watch. The meeting had been underway for twenty-one minutes. It was time for him to intervene, time to try once again to assert his view. He was sure that by virtue of his position as team leader and the force of his personality, he could make the discussion finally go his way.

He cleared his throat. "Look, people," he announced. "I want to say something here." A few faces turned in his direction, but the others looked straight ahead or down at their papers. "What we have to do," he went on as forcefully as he could, "is to find a solution that's right for the customer. The customer is number one. So I want to restate my position. The customer wants *more* features, not less. You guys are headed down the wrong path."

He sat back, expecting agreement. It didn't come.

"Hey, folks," he said, a faint note of desperation audible through his self-assurance and attempted humor. "I know what I'm talking about. I *am* the marketing guy here, and this is a marketing issue."

The people at the table waited in embarrassed silence until they saw that Mike was finished. Then they resumed their discussion about which product features could be dropped and still keep the customer happy.

Mike was stunned. They were treating him as if he'd said something very out of place. He tried to maintain his composure, but inside he was anxious, his chest was tightening. He'd been snubbed and ignored like this at several of the meetings. Had he lost his touch? What was happening here? Why weren't they listening? For the first time in his life he began to have thoughts of failure. What if, under his leadership, the team came up short? He'd be nailed for letting down the company in its time of crisis, and for disappointing the boss who'd given him this chance.

Several months before, when it had become clear that the firm's competitors were ravaging its markets, Mike's boss, the vice president of marketing, had decided it was time for a radical approach. Friends of his who were executives at other companies had given him glowing reports of how effective cross-functional teams could be in speeding up product development. The concept was sweeping the business world. Many management experts hailed it as the only way for a company to organize if it wanted to compete effectively.

Typically, these teams were composed of employees from a variety of company divisions, such as research and development, marketing, and production, along with representatives from the firm's suppliers and occasionally its customers. Team members came together as equals, not as superiors and subordinates, and together they shaped decisions from the very start of a new product.

This contrasted markedly with the way decisions used to be made. In the past, each division took charge of a certain phase of a product's development, handing it off to the next division. Research and development might suggest the initial idea. Engineering would design it. Manufacturing would make it. Marketing and sales would find the customers for it. This traditional approach—passing work sequentially from one department to the next—took considerable time. One group's work could be drastically revised by the next group, which stirred up resentment and caused inefficiencies.

Mike's boss had persuaded the company to try the cross-functional technique. Then he named Mike, his protégé, as the team's formal leader. The job, he knew, would give Mike important new management experience and high visibility in the company, setting him up for a major advancement.

Mike's team's first assignment was to hustle along the Personal Digital Assistant. The product had been languishing for more than a year in the research department. Now it was given top priority. If handled right, it could turn the company around. Mike knew that as leader of the team that accomplished the coup, he'd be springboarded into the executive suite.

That's how things looked to Mike when he signed on. Instead the opportunity was fast becoming a nightmare.

From the first meeting the team process had been difficult for Mike. He'd managed subordinates successfully for fourteen years, but this team was something else, especially the younger people. They'd seemed a lot harder to motivate.

His customary procedure in meetings had always been to begin by inviting everyone to participate in the decision making. His theory was that if you involved people to a point, they'd let you have your own way. Sure, it was a manipulation. He didn't care that much about getting their input. He was going through the motions. The gambit usually had worked for him. He'd been able to direct decisions in the end.

So in this, his first experience with the cross-functional team approach, he'd used the same tactic. At the initial meeting he'd gone around the table asking for views, and then he'd declared his own. That should have been that. But, for some reason, it wasn't. In the next forty minutes the group systematically plucked away many of the features Mike had earnestly promoted. It was as if he'd never spoken.

Mike felt he had to do something to turn this group around. If he didn't reestablish himself as the leader, he'd be disgraced. It was time, he told himself, to lay down the law. His career, after all, was on the line.

He squared his shoulders and placed both hands on the table. Just as his hands touched the wood, there was a lull in the conversation, and he moved quickly to take advantage of it.

"Okay," he said, "hold on just one minute. We're getting way off track. I want you guys to listen up for a minute." The expressions on the faces seemed less than receptive. "I am the team leader here. And Peter," he said, turning toward Peter, "I think you are just plain wrong. This is *not* a cost issue. You're going to kill this product before it ever gets out the door if you nickel-and-dime it with costs."

As he continued he gradually raised his voice. "We *have* to add features. Look, I want to go over again what customers are telling us. Remember what I said earlier about the focus groups. . . ."

The team sat patiently as Mike explained his perspective point by point.

"And that," he said emphatically in closing, "is what we've got to do."

Once again there was a pause, and then the conversation resumed its previous course, the course that Peter had set. It was as if Mike had never spoken. Baffled, slightly panicked, he asked himself what was wrong. He'd been a leader all his life. In high school he'd been class president, in college the head of his fraternity. At the company he had won promotion after promotion. Now, it seemed, he couldn't even run a meeting. Maybe he'd just been lucky all his life and now his luck was running out.

As he looked around the room, he reminded himself that no one here was his subordinate. Few of these people had a vested interest in his leadership, let alone his career. His formal title didn't make much difference to them either. These people were more or less his peers. How could you lead people if they were your equals? It seemed a contradiction.

His mind raced through the handful of management books he had recently read. None of them had talked about leading in this type of situation.

His reflections were interrupted by a voice at the far end of the table. "It's six P.M.," the person said. "Time to adjourn?" There were murmurs of assent.

Someone else named several members of the team who might collect more information before the next meeting, and those members said they would.

"And Mike," a third person said, "why don't you bring more of your research results?" Mike wondered for an instant if the suggestion was meant to rub his nose in his bungle, then realized it was sincere. He nodded, slowly lifted himself, and turned toward the door.

That night was a restless one for Mike. It took him a long time to drop off, and when he awoke, the red digital numbers on his clock said 4:23 A.M. He knew he couldn't get back to sleep, so, trying not to disturb his slumbering wife, he got out of bed and went down to the kitchen. For an hour he sat at the kitchen table analyzing the catastrophe of the day before, trying to puzzle out a plan of action. He finally decided to go see his friend Frank Freeman and ask for advice. He knew Frank came in early, so he'd get there early, too.

Frank was vice president of manufacturing, and as such he was Peter's superior. He was at his desk when Mike came by, and he greeted Mike with a cheery smile. Fatigue in his voice, Mike began explaining the problems he was having with the team and with Peter.

After a few minutes, Frank interrupted. "Mike," he said, "I'm going to tell you something very candidly. Please don't take it personally. The basic problem is your style."

"My *style?*" Mike said.

"Yes, your style. You're used to ordering people around, commanding them to make things happen. Sure, you go through the motions of inviting discussion, but you've got to admit you really prefer calling most of the shots."

"Well, somebody's got to be in charge," Mike said.

"Yes, but not in quite the way we used to do it. It's different now. Times are changing, and Peter's the new breed."

"And I'm the old breed, I suppose," Mike said, "at forty-five."

"You're not old," Frank said, "you've just been doing things the old way. And you've been lucky because your staff knows you and likes you, so they tolerate it. But most people won't. Peter's figured out that people today want to be persuaded into action, not commanded. He's not one bit smarter than you, but he's gotten very good at convincing and motivating groups."

"He is good," Mike admitted. "I don't know how he does it."

"He's learned the art of listening to others," Frank said, "and then he takes their viewpoints and suggestions and incorporates them into his solutions. Which is great because his solutions then resonate with everyone."

"Well, he certainly does do that."

"Yes, he does. And have you noticed that he's also very creative when it comes to finding compelling evidence for something? I heard about that one meeting you guys had where Peter brought in the outside consumer marketing expert—of all things—to talk about why 'value-driven' consumers didn't want more features. That was a masterstroke—right on your own turf."

"Yeah, it was," Mike said.

"Heck, even I've been learning some things from him," Frank said, smiling. "You would not believe the buy-in I'm starting to get for projects that in the past would have been a complete up-hill sell. I guess I'm finding there are better ways to get things done today rather than to steam-roll them through."

"Tell me about it," Mike said, now smiling with Frank. "It's the steam-roller who gets flattened."

What Is Persuasion?

Quite simply, *effective persuasion is the ability to present a message in a way that leads others to support it.*[1]

For example, if I have presented my arguments effectively in this book and have shown truly convincing evidence, then when you finish reading it you should find yourself freely choosing to support my assertion—that persuasion is a critical management skill. You will also believe that you came to that conclusion by means of your own judgment, not by my forcing, tricking, or negotiating you into that belief.

If you support my assertion, it will mean that I have successfully done my homework about your needs. You will feel that I have accurately understood certain dilemmas you face today, and that I have provided a useful solution to them. I have persuaded you effectively.

Real persuasion creates a sense of freedom for the listener: the freedom to choose.[2] This is in contrast to being commanded or negotiated into something. For example, imagine if I ordered you to believe in the ideas in this book: "Listen here, this book portrays reality! Accept it or else!" Or if I tried to negotiate a deal with you: "Look, you agree to the ideas in my book, and I will agree to the ideas in your next book, okay? Is that a deal?"

Which approaches are likely to have a successful impact on you? I think you'd agree that persuasion would be more influential than the direct order or the deal making. It's because effective persuasion makes you feel, and rightly so, as if you chose to agree. You were not forced because I'm the boss or because we made a trade. The ideas made good sense, you saw advantages for yourself, and you jumped onboard.

Frank laughed. "Exactly. But it's not just a matter of giving up an old behavior and starting a new one. You can't just throw a switch and wham! you're a new-style manager. These techniques of Peter's can be subtle, and you've got to understand the principles involved."

Frank's secretary came into the outer office. She hung up her coat and pulled out her desk chair. People were now passing in the hall. The office day was beginning.

"But there are tradeoffs," Frank said, wrapping it up. "I'm learning that this new approach takes more of my patience and my willingness to compromise. But, you know something? It's worth it. I'm accomplishing a lot more this way."

He stood up and came around the desk and put his hand on Mike's shoulder. "Listen," he said. "You're a great guy and a talented executive. Once you get with this new approach, you'll be terrific. My advice is to do what I did. See how Peter does it and try it yourself. He's definitely onto something. Don't fight him, learn from him. We'd all better learn from him. I have this feeling that people like Peter will be the managers of the future."

Mike and Peter are very real people to me. I'm with them every day of my working life.

I'm a professor of management at the University of Southern California. I'm also a consultant, and for more than a decade and a half I've spent a great deal of my time among executives on both sides of the chasm that has divided their world. I've encountered the Peter Keenes, the executives who are in tune with this radical redefinition of leadership, and I've met the Mike Jacobsons, the old-style command executives who are on the outside looking in.

My consulting and my research, in fact, have put me in touch with literally thousands of managers in all types of industries and all sizes of organizations. I've studied over forty companies and trained and consulted in another fifty or so. I've worked with a lot of these firms for many years, so I've been able to watch their evolution over time.

I've also had the chance to get at some of the factors underlying the change. As a professor and chairman of the Leadership Institute at USC, I meet leading thinkers from around the world.

Together we've penetrated these trends that are slowly but fundamentally reshaping how managers lead and influence others—the trends that are lifting and propelling the Peter Keenes of this world.

It started about ten years ago. It was then that I began noticing that teams were becoming popular among companies that wanted to address problems more speedily. Soon afterward, clients began asking me for help because their more traditional managers, people such as Mike, were having trouble leading these groups. I watched as, over and over, command-style managers produced poor team outcomes.

The truth popped out at anyone who cared to look. Just because you were a stellar functional manager, working well within your division, it was no guarantee that you'd automatically be a good team leader. The dynamics of leading a team were just too different. Something more was needed than just functional expertise and directives.

I became fascinated by people such as Peter Keene, the rare individuals who are highly effective team leaders. Observing them I discovered that in contrast to other managers, they actually shied away from issuing directives. To get things done they depended instead on a deep understanding of the technique this book will impart: modern persuasion, along with its components such as mutual influence, building a consensus, developing relationships with people at their own level, and so on.

About the same time, I took on several companies that were getting their first Baby Boomer CEOs. In a number of cases, I had known the previous chief executives, so I could contrast the two generations. As I reflected on the Boomer executives I was getting to know, I started to see certain unique patterns in how they led. I realized I was observing a profound generational difference in how the new and old CEOs thought about leading and managing. Surprisingly, the Baby Boomer CEOs who had great impact shared many of the traits that I was observing among my effective team leaders. They were not command managers, but instead master persuaders.

In recent years, my work has also put me in touch with the youngest workplace generation, known as Generation X, after the title of a popular book about them. I've noted how these Xers

flourish under both effective team leaders and Boomer CEOs—
executives whose style relies far more than before on peer-based
managing, teamwork, and use of persuasion instead of commands.

I've also seen how the rapid spread of electronic technologies
is reinforcing this new way of managing, by providing more access
to everyone and to everything.

I was so impressed by the effectiveness of these new managers
that I began to study them. Along the way, I discovered that the
actual number of Peter Keenes out there is still quite small. Maybe
10 percent of managers are proficient at the new management
skills, and that includes both generations, the Boomers and the
Xers. Another 25 to 35 percent of managers are Mikes, trapped in
the command model (but not without hope of relearning!).

The rest of us, like Frank Freeman, are somewhere between
the two. We "in-betweeners" understand that new skills are
needed. We're motivated to learn. We've even halfway figured out
a few of the techniques ourselves. But we've found there's only so
much we can learn on our own and without understanding the
fundamental principles.

For the last several years I've gone searching for the best of
the Peter Keenes, on the theory that the best can teach us the
most. My aim has been simple—to figure out exactly what this
outstanding new breed of managers does and what the rest of us
can learn from them. Through extensive interviews and observa-
tion, I began to pick up their secrets. I discovered, in fact, a series
of specific techniques that they shared in common.

These skills and practices are presented over the course of this
book. With them you can equip yourself for a successful and very
rewarding career in the twenty-first-century world of business.

2
Persuasion:
The Six Killer
Myths

A colleague of mine, Lenn Greenlaugh of Dartmouth College, designed a classroom exercise to teach managers how to negotiate. I borrowed it to show the managers I train how wrong their ideas about persuasion can be.

Here's how it works. In a seminar with managers I choose six from the class and tell them they're vice presidents of a certain prominent corporation. (The rest of the managers will be onlookers.) Each of them, I say, runs a different function of the company —sales, marketing, manufacturing, and so forth. They're all members of a cross-functional team assigned to choose among some options.

I give each team member a three-page script telling what he'll be persuading. I tell him to memorize that script. The team members will never see one another's scripts.

Appointing myself the company's president, I describe the options the team must consider. Then I say: "Your job is to arrive at a *consensus* on which of a number of new options we should adopt to enhance our product line. Your goal is to reach the right business decision, a decision that is based on an *effective sharing and discussion of the facts.* You have ninety minutes to reach your decision."

Having gone through this exercise many times, always questioning the class members afterward, I know that all six vice presidents are going into the assignment with an expectation as to what will happen next. They're assuming that as a team they'll weigh the various perspectives rationally; they'll maximize the amount of information on the table; and then they'll persuade one another effectively until the best decision emerges.

Here's what happens instead.

Within the first five minutes, several vice presidents take stands, declaring their positions and explaining why these positions are the most reasonable. Typically, the sales and manufacturing vice presidents polarize because they represent the two extremes. One wants the most options, the other wants the least. As opinions emerge, the other participants start lining up, forming subgroups of like-minded teammates.

The team members' behavior changes. Some grow quiet and lean away from the table. Others plant their elbows firmly on the table and aggressively defend their positions.

As time passes, the vice presidents persuade less and less and argue more and more. Most become increasingly locked into their positions. Those with shared viewpoints tell each other just how right these shared opinions are. As the deadline for decision approaches, deal making begins. Certain individuals support others on one option in return for support on another option. This horse trading goes on until, finally, a "consensus" decision is reached.

The team members believe they've succeeded. They made the decision within the deadline. But I disabuse them. "You've failed," I say, "because your decision was not based on the *effective sharing and discussion of the facts* I called for. It's a forced solution, a standoff." When asked how much constructive persuasion was done, most express disappointment.

This exercise powerfully illustrates what most managers think you mean when you speak of persuasion. They see it as essentially a manipulative affair in which they set forth what they feel are the best arguments for their position and rely on dominance and gamesmanship to win the day. The truth is that when we use ploys like those to get our way, we violate the most fundamental rules of constructive persuasion.

Shift for a moment to your own company. Imagine a recent meeting in which most of the participants were peers and several of them held different opinions on the same issue. What do you recall about the way the discussion went? The chances are that you'll see some strong parallels to Lenn Greenlaugh's exercise. You'll realize that many of your colleagues—and perhaps you yourself—share very similar views of persuasion. To them,

1. persuasion is simply *mustering the best arguments* for something;
2. persuasion almost always involves *stating your position up front;*
3. persuasion means *being assertive*—often very assertive; and
4. *negotiating and deal making* are at the heart of it.

These are some of the stereotypes people have about the act of convincing. There are several others. Together I call them the "killer myths" of persuasion—"killer" because they can kill our ability to be effective and our motivation to become better persuaders.

Myth Number One: The Most Effective Persuasion Is the Hard Sell

This is the most widespread of the myths. It is based on the John Wayne School of Persuasion. You stride into the meeting, strongly state your position at the outset, and then shoot off as many arguments as possible. Everybody cheers, and they make you sheriff.

In this scenario, persuasion is essentially a hard sell. You develop a good idea and get some evidence to support it. Then, by a process of logic, persistence, and personal enthusiasm, you sell others on the idea. Your success depends on taking bold stands and making your position irresistible. Even exaggerated claims are okay to make your point. When contrary positions are proposed by others, you simply shoot these down with a negative comment or two in hopes of making your ideas look even better. You come out of the meeting and your secretary asks how you did, and you say, "I knocked 'em dead."

This is what I see many managers do when they attempt to persuade. Here's an example of a hard-sell persuasion I attended.

A group of automobile executives are debating whether to deploy a less expensive V-6 engine as a substitute for an existing V-8 in a top-of-the-line model. The group includes the vice presidents of corporate planning, production, sales, marketing, and R & D:

> *VP of Planning:* I feel very strongly about using the V-6. It's a fully proven engine. We'll have tremendous economies of scale between the various product lines. And my hunch is that once it's turbo-charged, few customers will know the difference between it and the V-8.
>
> *VP of R & D:* Well, there's a problem with that engine, which is that it can't grow technically. It's reached its limit. Performance will be limited for years to come.
>
> *VP of Planning:* But it's already developed and proven as an engine! With turbo-charging, it can be just as hot.
>
> *VP of R & D:* But you can't grow it. We need an engine that will grow with the future.
>
> *VP of Planning:* You guys in R & D aren't concerned enough about the cost issues, though. We've got serious cost problems we need to solve. Whether the engine can grow is not terribly relevant.
>
> *VP of R & D:* Well, I totally disagree.
>
> *VP of Marketing:* I've also got some concerns about a V-6. It is simply not going to fit our image of a high-performance car. We need to stick to the V-8.

VP of Sales: I'd side with you [VP of Marketing] on the V-8 because we've got to differentiate this product. Our mission is to have an innovative, distinctive product that people will pay for. We don't want to make Russian Ladas.

When the vice president of corporate planning opened the meeting with his strong stand in favor of the V-6, he accomplished exactly the opposite of what he'd really intended. He'd wanted to win support for his position. Instead he provoked the other vice presidents to take immediate strong stands against him. The result was a stalemate: The two sides dug in and stopped listening to each other. The V-6 proposal was tabled.

The night before that meeting, the vice president of corporate planning probably spent the evening with his head in his briefcase, boning up for the big confrontation. What he should have done instead was to take his family to the circus. The circus? Absolutely. Sitting there in his box seat, munching his caramel popcorn, he should have kept a close eye on the lion tamer standing in the center ring, facing down the gigantic, snarling lion.

Lion tamers know something about their adversary that the vice president did not know about his. They know that a lion is programmed to attack in a certain way. It wants to pounce on its prey so that its paws and legs wrap firmly around the creature's torso. That's so it has something substantial to hold on to while biting its prey to immobilize it.

So how do lion tamers put that knowledge to use? The vice president would have noticed that as the tamer defied the lion, he held out an ordinary wooden chair with its legs pointing at the lion. The lion would have liked to pounce, but the chair ruined everything. There was no mass to clutch on to, nothing to grab, just the air between the thin chair legs, which meant the lion would have had no way to stabilize itself as it tried to pounce on the trainer. If it had pounced it would have lost its balance and fallen to the ground.

A similar phenomenon happens when we persuade. If we throw out a strong position at the start of a meeting, we are offering potential opponents a target, a solid mass to grab on to. On the other hand, if we wait a bit before stating our position until we've developed some sense of what's on the other participants' minds, and if we are somewhat indirect as we set forth our position, perhaps phrasing it as a question or even allowing someone else to present it, we are offering potential opponents the lion tamer's chair. There's not much to grab on to.

The strong, up-front sell makes people feel that we are trying to dominate them. They take it as a challenge, not an invitation. Automatically they shift into a defensive state I call the "counter-persuasion" mindset. Instantly they start generating opinions to counter ours. The participants divide into two camps—those who support us and those who don't. Persuasion then becomes an up-hill battle. The persuader's enthusiasm becomes suspect. Listeners are uncomfortable, feeling they're being sold too hard.

Returning to the V-6 example, a more effective approach would have been to pose the V-6 issue as a question framed around the company's objectives of profitability and future growth—objectives no one could argue with. Rather than opening like General George S. Patton standing on top of an M-16 tank, the VP of planning could have held back, chosen his moment, and then said: "Listening to the talk around this table, I sense there's some concern about our cost structure over the coming years. I'm completely with you on that one. We're all aware that the Japanese have made manufacturing costs their number one issue.

"In that connection I've found myself wondering lately if there might be some initiatives related to our engines that we could mutually explore here together—initiatives that could help us as a company. Anybody else here been thinking along those lines?"

If the vice president of planning had gone about things this way, he'd have created an opportunity for others in the group to propose the V-6 or another attractive alternative. If after a reasonable time no one else did, then he could have done it himself, but in the context of a free-ranging discussion in which a number of people had had a chance to air their views. He wouldn't have come off, counterproductively, as Mr. Heavy. Instead of resistance he would have met with receptivity.

And his gains wouldn't have ended there. Having heard the views of those in the room *before* he spoke, he'd have known in advance who his potential supporters were and what approaches might work best in getting them to share ownership with him in the V-6 proposal. He also might have picked up remarks that gave him some clues about coping with his opponents.

The hard-sell manager cheats himself of flexibility and fore-knowledge. With issues as fundamental as the one in the V-6 discussion, a manager really needs to assess—beforehand—the strength of his relationships with possible opponents to see how firmly and openly he can present his position. He should explore the other participants' positions on the issue before the meeting. If he does, he may find points of support or compromise that will open the group to a consideration of his ideas and his larger objectives.

Like so many managers I've encountered, the vice president of planning came on strong with his V-6 proposal, and it flopped. Don't fall for the hard-sell myth. Hard sell rarely works. If you come on strong, you go out weak.

Myth Number Two: Persuasion Is a One-Way Process

Many people, like the V-6 VP above, think of persuasion as selling —making a pitch, the way you might pitch a proposal to a client in a formal presentation. That kind of selling is a one-way process: Here's why you should buy what I've got; take it or leave it.

True persuasion isn't a one-way process. Professor Kathleen Reardon of the University of Southern California's School of Business likes to point out that a good persuader rarely changes another person's behavior or views without altering his own in the process.[1] At the heart of successful persuasion there is a continuous feedback loop from our audience to ourselves. To persuade meaningfully, we must not only listen to the other person and understand his point of view; we must also incorporate his perspectives in our arguments. And we must do it in a manner that allows him to feel that we have positively responded to his needs.

One company I have studied extensively, a manufacturer of jet engines, has been experimenting with cross-functional teams.

In the jet engine business, design engineers are considered the high-status experts because they can conceptualize extremely complex engine designs. As a result, they're often appointed the leaders of their teams. Some use their status to dominate the others on the team. Some, but not all.

The company's most successful team was led by a young engineer. During his first team meeting he noticed that the manufacturing representatives were unusually quiet. He made some discreet inquiries around the company and discovered that the manufacturing people felt their function was low status, so they tended to defer to the high-status design engineers. Our young team leader became concerned. He was afraid that if the manufacturing representatives stayed silent, they'd fail to contribute important insights essential to the success of the project.

He explained the situation to me: "Early on, I learned that manufacturing looks up to engineering, but they're a bit scared of us. So it's hard for them to contest our designs. We engineers gave them very close tolerances on everything, but we didn't tell them why. They just did what we said, without question. That was my dilemma. I was getting so little feedback from them."

Two days after the first team meeting, the young team leader headed out to the shop floor of the manufacturing operations. "At first," he said, "it was hard to communicate. I had to convince the manufacturing guys that I wasn't just a typical design engineer. I had to change their image of my role, and I had to do it one-on-one. I had to strip away the status barriers that have kept engineering and manufacturing at arm's length and closed down the information flow.

"For example, the stress expert on the team [an engineer] might say, 'I need thirty hours of stress testing on the engine blade.' I could see the manufacturing guy look downward as if to say he didn't have the time to run such a long test. But I knew he wouldn't come out and say that in the meeting. And I felt that if I called on him in the meeting and tried to get him to say it, it would embarrass him and he'd clam up.

"When I went down to the manufacturing department, I wouldn't tell them what we had to have, I'd ask for their help. I'd pull down my tie and say, 'What's the best you can do? You tell me if it's too difficult.' I'd have three manufacturing guys there so that they could bunch up on me and tell me their honest feelings in confidence.

"We set up a minicourse for the manufacturing people on the engineering issues of the engine blade, so the engineers could voice their concerns. Then we asked manufacturing to give us engineers a tour of manufacturing and to give us a minicourse. In other words, we built a higher level of interaction, with the result that we saved $2 million alone in standardizing parts.

"Basically, I achieved this through persuasion and relationship building. I didn't sell my ideas or those of others through a lot of directives but through a tremendous amount of dialogue and convincing and relationship building."

As Professor Reardon emphasizes, effective persuasion always involves a chain of feedback. We must show that the steps we are urging have value for others. If our coworkers are not persuaded, it means that we have failed to understand their needs and concerns.

So, contrary to its popular image, persuasion is not about finding gullible listeners or seductive arguments to be swallowed whole. It's more a mutual search for solutions that offer advantages both to the persuader and to the persuadee. Both sides have to see the positives for themselves in what is being proposed.

What many managers do, however, is to persuade strongly from their own viewpoint alone. They can see the benefits so clearly; surely, they think, the person they're talking to can see them, too, just the way they see them, and appreciate them. This, alas, is rarely the case.

Myth Number Three: Effective Persuaders Succeed on the First Try

Many managers I have interviewed assume that if you're a good persuader, you usually succeed with an audience on the first or second try. So naturally when they themselves don't promptly succeed, they see it as a personal failure and conclude they don't have what it takes.

The fact of the matter is that even for the best of persuaders, the path of true persuasion, like true love, doesn't always run smoothly. Research on persuasion reveals that persuasion, like romance, often requires an ongoing effort.[2] A successful act of persuasion typically runs like this:

1. At the first meeting, we convince a few of our teammates simply to consider our perspective more carefully.
2. At the second meeting we win several of them over to our viewpoint, but only after we make certain alterations in our own position.
3. The following week, events outside our control unravel some of our efforts or, possibly, bolster them.
4. Successive meetings and discussions eventually bring all the members of our team to agreement and support. Along the way, we keep making adjustments in our position. (We might even be converted to a new position ourselves!)

Unfortunately, there is no way to speed up this process. Even the best persuaders I know have to tread this same trail, must go with this same flow. Even the best of them seldom has an idea that wins everyone over on the first or second try. Adaptability and persistence are what get them through, not hypnotism.

Myth Number Four: Good Persuaders Don't Need to Compromise

For command managers, compromise is hell. If they can't have it exactly their way, it's an insult to their mastery. Even for most of the rest of us, needing to compromise seems a sign of weakness.

Let's set the record straight. Compromise is an essential part of persuasion. Compromise is not the opposite of persuasion but its ally.

What we're dealing with here is the buy-in process. Before people buy into our proposal, they want to see that we're willing to make some changes, some sacrifices, in response to their needs and concerns. Making concessions to our audience is a way for us to show them respect. The unspoken message conveyed through an act of compromise is: "I respect you, and I am taking your wishes very seriously." It also brings another powerful dynamic into play: If we give them something of value, it creates a sense of obligation on their part. They will feel they owe us something in return.

We think of compromise as a weakness only because it is so often forced on us. We should be ready to make judicious compromises, but we often are not. Instead, we are all caught up in our own wishes, our own drives to score. So when compromise finally becomes strategically unavoidable, it has to be rammed down our throats. We could have felt successful; instead, we feel shamed.

The effective persuader always considers ahead of time what the needs of others might be and knows the areas where he may have to compromise. This is essential homework for a manager, but most managers don't bother. When they are called upon to compromise, they are caught off guard.

For the effective persuader, compromise is an essential tool. Sometimes, however, you may wish not to compromise. In such cases, simply recognize the risk that your position may not gather the amount of commitment it needs.

Myth Number Five: Great Arguments Are the Secret to Successful Persuasion

A stereotype that blocks many of us from seeing our potential as persuaders is the mistaken belief that effective persuasion depends almost entirely on dazzling arguments and stupendous ideas. We imagine that the best persuaders must be special geniuses who are able to consistently think up foolproof positions that instantly convince. "If only I was that smart!" we think to ourselves.

Here's the reality. Finding a persuasive position in management takes a great deal of effort and experimentation. Rarely, if ever, is it possible to arrive at one on the first try. More often than not, we must test our positions, develop new ones, retry, involve others in refining them, and then try again. Extensive experiments may be needed to find solutions and compromises that will leave colleagues feeling that they themselves have freely chosen to adopt a position.

Good persuaders, therefore, tend to be very curious people. Professor Reardon explains: "The most persuasive people listen, empathize, negotiate, motivate, and reward skillfully. These people select strategies with the needs and desires of the persuadee in mind. They know that just as the perfect gift is not something the giver would like for himself but something the recipient would prize, so too the most effective persuasion strategies are the ones responsive to the interests of the persuadee."[3]

Good arguments are of course a part of effective persuasion, but other factors are often just as important. For example, the degree of trust we've developed (or failed to develop) with our audience can be as influential as the quality of our arguments.

Myth Number Six: Persuasion Is Pure Manipulation

Many of us shrink from persuasion. The very word has negative connotations for us. It makes us think of the hard-charging car salesman or the wily politician or the deal-hustling stockbroker. The word *manipulation* automatically springs to our minds. This misconception keeps us from learning to be effective persuaders. We don't want to be seen as manipulators.

A colleague and friend, John Kotter, a professor at the Harvard Business School, set out a decade ago to study power in organizations. What he discovered was that many managers were naïve about power. Some played down its importance. Others dismissed its use as manipulative. Kotter found that those managers who shied away from power proved to be less effective and less successful. He also discovered, on the other hand, that there were many uses of power that were actually positive forces within organizations.

The same, I'm convinced, is true of persuasion. Just like power, it can be used to help others and ourselves, or it can be highly self-serving and harmful. There is a positive side, and there is a negative side. My objective in this book is to show you how to be far more effective at what I call constructive persuasion.

Manipulative persuasion is self-serving. The goal is to cop benefits for ourselves. The needs of colleagues and the best interests of the organization don't come into the picture. We might rationalize our motive and emphasize the potential for colleagues; but in reality we're the only ones who stand to gain, and we know it. In short: If the intent of your pitch is to deceive or to harm someone, then it is clearly manipulative. This is the lowest form of persuasion.

In contrast, constructive persuasion serves not only ourselves but others. The outcome is always geared to the best solution for everyone involved. This form of persuasion is not a process of pulling the wool over the eyes of others through clever arguments or misleading information. Nor is it an adversarial game in which we manage to get our own way with minimal compromise. It depends on listening sensitively to others, so that we can find a common ground of shared needs and perspectives.

When we are using this approach to persuasion, we are essentially creating a dialogue, a contest for effective ideas, a synthesis of the very best ideas, and then crafting them into convincing positions that can be widely agreed to. This is what our young jet-engine engineer did. He created and then managed a process for synthesizing and promoting the ideas of his team, including his own ideas, to get the best answer. He is a great example of constructive persuasion.

One way to tell what kind of persuasion you're involved in is to look at the evidence you're using. Manipulative persuasion usually employs misleading evidence.

A second test is to see how direct you're being. Even constructive persuasion has a strongly tactical side and at times relies on approaches that are not always up front. But that's true of most human communications; nearly every exchange with others involves some measure of indirectness, and for good reason.[4] Human contact quickly breaks down without some measure of tact and discretion. If we all were instantly candid with each other, nothing much would ever get done, except war.

To be effective, persuasion often depends on subtlety and

roundabout approaches. It will also involve skillful and deliberate timing; decisions must be made about *when* to share one's views or information. Tact is almost always required, in order to avoid hurting feelings or to allow the other person to save face. In Japan, the extreme example, communications must be indirect. Rarely would a Japanese directly and emotionally confront another, especially in a public setting. Every culture has its own concept of the proper ratio between candor and tact. It varies within regions and cities and from one company to the next. You have to tune your communication according to where you find yourself or ears will shut to what you are proposing.

How do we know when our persuasion slips into the manipulative and unethical because it is not up front? Social scientist Robert Cialdini, an expert on how people influence each other, has identified what he calls "triggers of influence." Triggers are the rewards or appeals that encourage the persuadee to be persuaded. Cialdini suggests that it's the way the persuader crafts these triggers that determines whether or not his persuasion is ethical.[5]

Constructive persuaders find triggers that are truly present in the situation at hand. For example, a real estate salesman might highlight a home's new plumbing or how close the schools are. Manipulative persuasion occurs when the triggers are fabricated to convince—in other words, not naturally present in the situation. For example, the real estate salesman tells you that the school board has decided to build a school near your prospective home, yet in reality no such decision was made. Or a male actor who has a full head of natural hair appears on television to promote a hair growth cream. Both bring into the persuasion situation characteristics or "facts" that are not real or truthful.[6] Omissions of certain facts can also be unethical if they seriously mislead.

Constructive and ethical persuasion does not always mean sharing everything you know up front.[7] As we saw in our discussion of the auto engine debate, sometimes effective persuaders prefer not to state their position until later in the process. But ethical persuasion does require our statements to be truthful to the best of our knowledge, and that we not make them when their reliability is in doubt.

Here are some basic tips to help you tell whether your own

persuasion is manipulative or constructive. Simply ask yourself the following questions:

1. Who will really benefit as a result of this act of persuasion? Is it largely me or will important benefits go to my colleagues?

    If it is largely you, then it's probably manipulative persuasion. To shift to the constructive side, you should alter your position so that it really does something significant for those you're persuading.

2. Is the information I am presenting reliable or is it misleading and inaccurate?

    If you know it's misleading and unreliable, you are engaged in manipulative persuasion. It's better to substitute honest and accurate information or to say you don't know what the facts are.

3. Does my persuasion on this issue feel like a competitive game and test of wills or a healthy dialogue and positive debate?

The more persuasion feels like a competition, the more likely it is that you're some distance from constructive persuasion. The goal is to be as inclusive as you can, to bring out information and stimulate discussion, then zero in on appealing solutions.

Those are the six killer myths about persuasion. The exceptional persuaders I have known all broke away from these popular misconceptions. Don't let them get in your way as you experiment with the techniques ahead.

The Components of Successful Persuasion

Now that we know what persuasion *isn't*, we may be wondering what constructive persuasion really *is*. There are four distinct steps to becoming an effective persuader, and each of the next four chapters discusses one of them. Here's a preview.

Building Your Credibility

The first hurdle we face as persuaders is the question of credibility. Our listeners are asking themselves: "Can we trust this person's viewpoint on the issue at hand?" Sometimes the hurdle is even higher, and listeners wonder if they can trust the person himself.

This is a normal reaction. Allowing oneself to be persuaded involves some risk, after all. You're putting yourself in the persuader's hands, in a sense. So it's essential that our colleagues feel that both we and what we're proposing are credible. Any doubts will undermine their confidence in the validity of our position and make it harder for them to agree to it. The foundation of effective persuasion is our credibility.

Finding the Common Ground

Credibility is not enough. You might have a high degree of credibility with your colleagues, yet if what you're proposing doesn't connect with their own interests, your message will fall on deaf ears. Persuasion often fails because people either tune us out or go on the defensive when they feel that we are trying to persuade them to *our* viewpoint, especially when it is not *their* viewpoint. As persuaders, we can never assume that our listeners understand the advantage to them of what we are trying to persuade them to do.

The next step is the search for shared ground. We need to understand what our colleagues are expecting, what they are concerned about, and what they are feeling. Then we must demonstrate that what we're trying to persuade them of is of shared concern both to them and to us. Only in this way can we gain not only their interest but their agreement.

Developing Compelling Positions and Evidence

Shared advantages, however, are not sufficient unless they're backed up by compelling positions and evidence.

To arrive at the point where we ourselves are prepared to persuade, we typically have gone through a process of self-convincing, involving some personal research and reflection. We emerged from this process with a vivid sense of the key points and the data that convinced us. But the things that convinced us may not be the same things that will convince others.

The third step, therefore, is to think carefully about our co-workers and decide what types of evidence they will find compelling. Your evidence should make clear how advantageous for them the course you are recommending will be. It should build their confidence that the outcomes you are predicting will actually occur or be delivered. Why should they invest if the return will not be realized? Our evidence must be quite convincing on this dimension.

Connecting Emotionally

Our colleagues want to see that we're emotionally committed. This type of commitment—of the heart, not just the brain—is intimately connected to credibility. It shows as nothing else can that we are deeply connected to our position. For many, the emotions are the ultimate test of commitment.

When you set out to persuade, ask yourself: Do my emotions, my excitement, my own sense of urgency convey my commitment to what I'm proposing? If they do, they'll help motivate others into an enthusiastic endorsement of what we're proposing. Think about it: Have you ever seen people follow an unenthusiastic leader?

Colleagues will also want to see if our position connects emotionally with their concerns and aspirations. Ask yourself: Does my persuasion address my colleagues' emotional feelings about the situation? Does it speak to their aspirations? Does it address their fears? When you connect to their emotions, your persuasion will have great appeal.

In the chapters to follow, you'll see why all four of the components I've just described are so critical to successful persuasion and how they link to one another. To illustrate each of them, I'll draw upon actual case examples showing how real managers performed on these different dimensions, effectively or poorly. Then I'll offer you techniques that will help you perform well.

Table 1
The Four Elements of Effective Persuasion

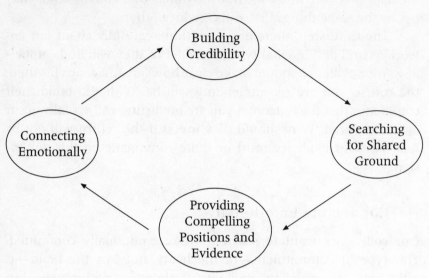

3
Building Credibility for Ourselves

We've seen how many managers confuse persuasion with taking bold stands and aggressive arguing. When I've interviewed their colleagues afterward, I've discovered that time and time again this type of action triggered a "counterpersuasion" mindset in their audiences. The strong stands were interpreted as highly self-serving. The persuader's coworkers asked themselves, in effect: "Is this person truly interested in the impact of his ideas on my responsibilities and career?" Their responses were usually "no." A strong stand evoked these reactions even when the persuader demonstrated a concern for others. Invariably such actions raised questions about the persuader's *credibility*.

Credibility is the starting point for effective persuasion. It is a critical factor, since persuasion most often takes place in situations where there are no clear answers, where interpretations of the issues diverge, and where evidence is conflicting. In these circumstances, where no one perspective or argument is seen as clearly superior to others, we tend to turn to the person whose expertise we believe in, given the issue at hand.

Aristotle, the ancient Greek philosopher, is considered the

father of the art of persuasion. He was the first to codify its laws in a comprehensive manner. Credibility, he wrote, was the principal source of a persuader's influence. He defined it in terms of one's character. "The character of the speaker," he wrote, "is a cause of persuasion, for as a rule we trust men of probity [integrity and uprightness] more, and more quickly, about things in general, while on points outside the realm of exact knowledge, where opinion is divided, we trust them absolutely. . . . [Credibility is] the most potent of all the means of persuasion."[1]

For this very reason, you should start any act of persuasion with this question: "Will I be perceived as credible on this issue?"

In work situations, we build our credibility around two factors: expertise and relationships. Whenever we attempt to persuade our coworkers, they make initial judgments about our credibility based on assessments of our expertise and our relationships. By finding ways to improve our position in both of these areas, we can become far more powerful persuaders.

Our coworkers judge our expertise by our history of sound judgments and by how knowledgeable they perceive us to be. To assess our soundness of judgment, our colleagues rely on qualities well described by Gerald Hauser, an expert on persuasion research:

> If we believe the person is well-informed, has studied a question thoroughly, is clearheaded and reasonable in their beliefs, is able to provide reasons and evidence in response to objections, does not utter foolish or exaggerated or asinine or banal opinions, is her own person and is not easily mislead, or has a special expertise through training or experience, we are likely to have confidence in their advice. Conversely, if a person is a sloppy reasoner or slow-witted or uninformed or given to extreme claims or is easily duped, our guard is raised to be cautious of her advice because it may not be thought out.[2]

Colleagues assess our knowledge partly according to our track record on similar issues and partly by our understanding of the specific issue being considered. If we are perceived as the most knowledgeable on the issue, that perception will go a long way toward winning us commitment.

When I began this book, I interviewed the president of one of Madison Avenue's hotter advertising agencies. He had made a name for his firm with "reality-style" advertising showing real people in eye-catching situations. For example, in his campaign for Ikea furniture, the advertisements showed a live-in couple shopping for furniture. What was unusual about the couple was that they were two men. The reality-style formula had proved quite successful, and at the time that I met him, his agency had won Tanqueray gin, Lens Crafter's opticians, Prudential Securities, and numerous other household names as accounts.

The pitching of advertising campaigns is a high form of the art of persuasion. The president had just come out of a new-client meeting, and I asked him how much persuasion he'd had to do. He said that thanks to his recent string of successful campaigns, he hadn't had to do much. His knowledge of what it took to create a successful campaign, in short, was doing most of the talking. And that's the way it goes. When there's a clearly acknowledged expert on an issue, extensive persuasion is often unnecessary.

We can't all be experts, of course, especially in the early stages of our careers or in a new job or project assignments. In many of the persuasion situations we are likely to find ourselves, our own experience and expertise will not be enough to win others immediately to our side. If they were, there would be no need for persuasion.

Consider this: Most discussions are held precisely *because* no single individual has all the solutions. The majority of circumstances at work require persuasion that incorporates differing points of view. Seldom is there one perspective clearly shared by all. Often the problem needs the input of multiple experts, each of whom understands only a portion of it. It is rare that the expertise of one person is so compelling and comprehensive that everyone quickly accedes to it. Otherwise there'd be far fewer meetings.

In addition, there remains the matter mentioned earlier—the issue of risk for our colleagues. If they look at our proposal and see high costs to themselves and few rewards, we could be the world's greatest expert and it wouldn't be enough to win their support.

● ● ●

On the relationship side of credibility, our reputation is influenced by whether we have built trusting and mutually beneficial relations. Perceptions of our integrity are critical. As we talk, our colleagues are evaluating our integrity not only by the amount we're displaying in our discussion of the matter at hand but by how we have demonstrated it in our past. In their opinion, has what we've espoused always matched up to what we've later done? Do they think of us as someone who always tells the truth and admits his mistakes? As someone who acts out of conviction, not expediency or opportunism? As someone concerned for others, or largely for himself?[3]

Candid answers to these questions will reveal our colleagues' perceptions of our integrity. Quite naturally, the more positive the assessment, the greater our perceived integrity.

Another major factor determining our relationship side of credibility is *emotional character*—the way people see us emotionally. Colleagues quite appropriately will ask themselves questions like this about you: Is he emotionally stable? Or does he tend to get enthusiastic about something one minute and bored with it the next? Is he intimidating and domineering or, to the contrary, is he submissive and lacking in conviction?[4]

The history of the way we've reacted emotionally to various situations influences our audiences powerfully. Like us, they tend to distrust individuals who are at emotional extremes. Colleagues are also looking to see if we are emotionally connected to them. Are we angry at the same things that they are angry about? On successful projects do we share in their enthusiasm and sense of "job well done"? Do we have an emotional and personal stake in what we are asking them to agree to, or is it just business to us? As we frame our own goals, do we have their interests at heart? The closer the emotional connection to colleagues, the more likely they'll be to come along with us.[5]

Together, these two factors—expertise and relationship—profoundly shape our reputation and in turn determine our credibility with any individual or group. It's crucial that we make an objective assessment of where we stand on both criteria before attempting to persuade others. Our strengths or weaknesses on either dimension will tell us important things about the persuasion approaches we need to employ.

It is important to remember that our coworkers' judgments are based on *their* perceptions, not ours. We may believe that we're an expert on an issue and that we have strong relationships. But it's not our perspective that counts. What counts is how our colleagues see us, and they may not share our perceptions. I have seen many managers who overestimated their reputations fail in their efforts to persuade.

Author Michael Crichton, known for books such as *Jurassic Park, The Andromeda Strain,* and *Terminal Man,* describes in his autobiography how perceptions of his credibility caused him difficulty early in his career as a movie director.

He had been chosen to direct a film entitled *The Great Train Robbery,* featuring Sean Connery and being filmed in Ireland. Crichton had come to Ireland directly from the experience of directing his first movie, *Coma,* which had just been released in the United States and was doing well. On the set in Ireland, the British film crew seemed unresponsive to his directing. When Crichton offered an idea, the crew invariably suggested alternatives—not out of conviction, he sensed, but to throw him off balance.

An assistant proposed to Crichton that the crew might enjoy seeing one of his films. Figuring that since *Coma* had only recently been released it would be hard to get a copy, Crichton didn't follow up on the suggestion. Several days later the assistant again proposed a viewing of the film. Again, Crichton, busy with the new job, didn't follow up. By then, however, problems with the crew had become much worse. Finally, the assistant insisted. "I really do think it would be nice," he said with some emphasis, "if the crew had a chance to view one of your films."

At that moment, Crichton realized what the assistant was really telling him. He was known to the crew only as an author. They had not had any direct experience of Crichton as a director. He quickly telephoned Hollywood and had a copy of *Coma* shipped overnight for a screening with the crew. The day after the screening Crichton's problems with the crew vanished. They had greatly enjoyed his film and now respected his decisions.[6]

It's critical that before you attempt to persuade you determine what your persuadees *actually* think of you. The techniques of assessing your credibility are covered in detail in the practice session at the end of this chapter (see page 65), but for the moment, use this simple method.

If we take the two dimensions of *perceived expertise* and *strength of relationships* and plot them onto a simple grid, we can chart our strengths and weaknesses and then diagnose what we need to do to enhance our credibility. For example, think of all the individuals you need to convince for an important upcoming issue. Then create a two-column table like Figure 1 (page 53) listing the names of each person you'll be persuading. For the column headings, put the labels "expertise" and "relationship." Using a simple scoring system of 1 to 5 (1 means you are very weak on that dimension; 5 means you are very strong on that dimension), rank how each person will perceive your overall expertise and relationship credibility. Now transfer your scores for each person over to a grid like Figure 2. Each of the four quadrants in which you place your individuals has different implications for how to best build credibility for that specific person. In the discussion to follow, I'll show you what steps you'll need to take for each quadrant. For example, if we're weak on the relational dimension, we might start building relationships with the individuals most likely to be making decisions on our proposals. (But we must be sincere in our attempts. Manipulative attempts are often easy to spot.) If we're short on expertise, we could turn to outside sources of expertise to make up for our weaknesses in this area.

What follows is a discussion of the three most difficult situations on the grid, with examples of how successful persuaders overcame personal limitations in each.

The fourth quadrant, identifying situations where both expertise and relationships are strong, has not been overlooked. If you find yourself in this happy situation, you can jump to the steps presented in the three chapters that follow. (But you won't want to miss learning the self-assessment techniques in the practice session at the end of this chapter. You may need them some day.)

Figure 1
Credibility Ratings

	EXPERTISE	RELATIONSHIP
Jackie	4	5
Turner	5	4
Brad	2	4
Lucy	4	2

Figure 2
The Credibility Quadrant

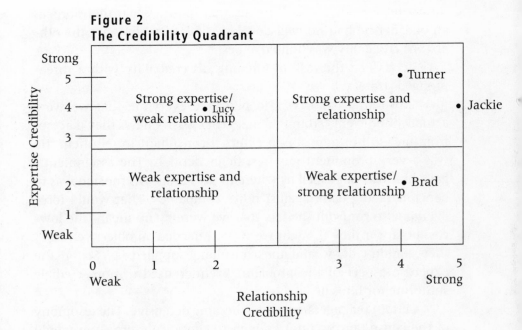

Weak Expertise and Weak Relationships

When we find ourselves with both meager expertise and weak relationships in the eyes of our colleagues, we are in the most difficult of the persuasion situations—poor credibility. So what to do? Here's what Tom Brenner did.

As the recently appointed chief operating officer of a large bank, Tom had to persuade his new colleagues that they had a serious problem: Overhead at the bank was excessive, he had learned, and would soon jeopardize the organization's competitiveness. Most of the staff believed that the bank's performance was superior to the competition's. Their attitude was: Why change a successful formula? But Brenner felt that a new competitive reality was upon the bank and that internal perceptions were distorted.

He also knew that when he made this argument, many at the bank would question his expertise. He had come from the financial investments community rather than retail banking. Why should they believe a newcomer from another industry? Furthermore, as an outsider he had no well-developed relationships with the others. His credibility was limited at best.

He tackled the task of building his credibility with a three-pronged strategy.

"My initial battle was to persuade everyone that we were actually inefficient," Tom told me. "That wasn't news they'd accept from me, so I brought in an external consultant to tell them. He was a very prominent guy, terrific credentials. The assignment I gave him was not to tell us where to save costs. His mission was to benchmark the bank against other companies. That would force everyone to confront the fact that we were by no means the low-cost producer they thought we were. I needed an objective reality they couldn't deny, and the consultant supplied it." So on the expertise aspect of the problem, Brenner used a more credible substitute for himself.

Certain managers, however, became defensive. The testimony of the consultant was not enough to convince them. Tom would have to work on them himself. Yet time was short; the bank would have to act soon. He could not wait for his relationships with these managers to build at the normal pace.

Carefully he calculated which managers would be most essential to the success of his change plan, the ones whose power would ultimately determine the fate of his initiatives. He began a series of visits with them to quickly create relationships and to win their trust.

> When I was brought to the bank, the message to me
> was, "This job is yours if it works, but if the team rejects

you then you're gone." So I said to myself, "Listen, no kidding here, I am running for office." How do you run for office in an organization? Well, in this case, I asked myself, "Where is the true power in this organization?" The true power is in the distribution system—the branches. So I got out and spent three months walking the branches, talking to people. I've seen every branch we have.

A lot of people thought that the power center was headquarters, but I said to myself, "No, no, if I have the distribution system saying that I'm their man, that I'm the first guy who actually understands what is going on, then I've got their trust." What happened was that I built up my credibility with this group in a relatively short time.

The real test, however, came when I had to answer questions back at headquarters. They were testing to see if I really understood issues in the field. Pretty soon people were saying to each other, "Wow, we can ask Tom about the retail branches, and he actually understands them."

Brenner's field visits demonstrated to staff in the branches that he was concerned about them. He cared enough to leave the corporate tower and spend months getting to know them. He wanted to understand their problems. This investment of time quickly enhanced the relational side of his credibility.

It also built his expertise. He was now an authority on issues facing the bank branches. Because he had surveyed so many of them, he now had the kind of broad perspective that few individuals even in senior management possessed. He was not only more expert; he was now that strongest of things, a unique expert. The personal interest in staff and the newly acquired knowledge made him more trustworthy and credible at the top level of the bank. He had successfully addressed his original gaps on the two credibility dimensions.

Brenner did one other thing. He sought out short-term opportunities to prove that his ideas were on target and further enhance perceptions of his expertise. He wanted to create several important early successes for himself.

Everybody wants tangible proof. Everybody likes instant results, and people are suspicious of waiting four years from now with nothing happening. So I needed some victories. So you go and you intervene in very particular ways. For example, we went into the retirement account season, and our staff would not have normally priced retirement accounts aggressively. I said that we were going to buy volume this season, and so we priced aggressively.

What you want to do is to intervene in tiny parts of the organization so the rest of the organization doesn't see that you've intervened. The goal is to deliver a victory. The volume in our mortgage business was slow, people were getting discouraged, so we needed a victory. Low-pay mortgage was my idea. I said, "Let's have a ninety-days no-pay mortgage." It worked. The mortgage business took off.

Tom Brenner's story shows how one individual can overcome the most difficult of the persuasion situations—low perceived expertise and weak relationships. It also shows that in most persuasion situations there is no simple shortcut. Effective persuasion usually means investing your time in building both your expertise and your relationships. It worked for Tom. His efforts not only woke up the bank but positioned it for far greater success. It is today ranked highest in customer service in its markets.

If, however, you've got the relationship links, you should of course put your efforts into enhancing perceptions of your expertise.

Weak Expertise and Strong Relationships

Consider this situation: You believe in a particular approach or solution but lack the depth of expertise to argue credibly for it. Or, in a variant of that, you find yourself urging an initiative that is new and unfamiliar to you and your organization. Either way, it's an expertise problem. Let's posit, however, that you have something going for you: Your relationships throughout the organization are strong enough to get a hearing.

One executive who found herself in just this situation is Karen Fries, a product-development manager at Microsoft.[7] Along with her partner, Barry Linnett, Karen was urging the development of a new software system. To be called BOB, it would use animated characters that gave tips to software users as they wrote letters, did home finances, recorded appointments, and dealt with other household tasks. The program's environment was a house with ten rooms. In each room there were objects that could be clicked to launch one of the eight different programs. For example, the wall calendar became the appointment book.

What would be unique about BOB was that it would have what is called a social interface to make users feel more at ease and in control. In place of traditional software menus and commands, there would be a dozen animated characters or "guides" who would interact "socially" with users in an environment that mimicked reality. They'd range from Java, an excitable dinosaur who drank coffee, to Hopper, a submissive rabbit with a lollipop. You'd choose the one you liked best and were comfortable with, and it would present you with options and tips as you were learning and using each program.

Around the company, BOB was considered a dubious venture. Software programmers typically looked down on anything involving cute little creatures. That sort of thing, they believed, was not "serious" software and would never sell. And there was evidence to support this view. Early experiments with cute characters had largely been unsuccessful. But Karen felt those experimental programs lacked the dynamism and complexity of BOB.

Her efforts in behalf of BOB went back to the fall of 1990. It was then she'd begun to feel that perhaps the time was right for a new direction in user-friendly software. She and Barry had been responsible for the development of a software suite called Microsoft Publisher. It was the company's first program to actively interact with users, asking them basic questions about what they wished to accomplish. Sensing the limitations of that program, Karen and Barry concluded that simply improving existing software approaches was not the way to tackle the issue. They also suspected that the home software market—a largely untapped market with few software standards—would be more open to radical innovation.

To initiate the project, Karen and Barry had to persuade Bill Gates, head of Microsoft, to allocate start-up resources. Securing resources for a new project at Microsoft is an arduous process. The company is filled with computer wizards who compete intensely for head count for their projects' initiatives. ("Head count" means the number of subordinates reporting to you.) Ultimately, it is this head count that determines if and when their software programs make it to the market.[8]

Karen and Barry kicked off the process with a memo to Gates. In this first memo, they argued that Microsoft needed to do something new to make using software easier. They also discussed the future of home software and suggested some tentative solutions to the problem of increasing benefits to users while lowering costs. They closed their memo by requesting a meeting with Gates to discuss the matter and to request thirty staff members to launch the initiative.

Thanks to prior interactions and projects, Karen and Barry had built a solid relationship with Gates. This won both of them an initial meeting with Gates. During their meeting, however, it became clear that Karen and Barry's expertise on the subject was still at a very basic level. So Gates sent them back to the drawing board with only two additional staff members.

After researching the problem in greater depth, they drafted a second memo to Gates. This one was a more detailed description of the problem. Using examples from studies of actual customers, they showed that many users were unaware of software features, even the main ones. At a follow-up meeting with Gates, they presented a development plan, videotapes of customers in focus groups, and some details on the new interface.

By this point they'd realized how effective characters on-screen could be in helping the users along. As Karen commented:

> Originally, we didn't know the importance of a social interface. We only started with a broad goal—of im-

proving user-friendliness with home applications—and later learned by just watching people how interested they were in a character. There was one point in our research where there's a little character in the show, in the home itself, and people started talking to it, getting excited. One guy grabbed my arm and said, "Tell Microsoft to keep the manuals, just give me this character to help me out!"

Gates was still not convinced. What Karen and Barry had been demonstrating to Gates was their expertise in understanding the problems of user-friendliness but not their expertise in finding the right solution. Karen explained:

> He [Gates] never communicated this with us at this time. But I think he thought, "This is a big idea with potentially a big payoff, but I'm not convinced these guys really know what they're talking about. . . . Karen and Barry have done good work in the past, but I need to have more evidence that they're going to accomplish what they set out to do."
> At the time we were very frustrated that Bill didn't give us the head count. Incredibly frustrated. We knew we'd be able to pull it off. Our whole focus at that point became—fine, we'll persuade them. Persuasion was everything, and it's something I love to do!

Aware of their need to overcome the lack of credibility on the expertise dimension, Karen and Barry set out to develop early prototypes of BOB as proofs of their ideas and their expertise. Gates himself had suggested they recruit a technical guru to build support for the project within Microsoft. So Karen got Darrin Massena, a programming expert who had worked on the Windows NT operating system, to join the team. Darrin's willingness to sign on impressed both Gates and the organization. In no time Darrin was devising intriguing prototypes of BOB.

During this period of experimentation, Karen and Barry attended a presentation given to the company's research group. Two

Stanford professors, Clifford Nass and Bryon Reeves, had been invited to speak on human interaction with computers. They had been testing human/computer interaction for a decade, applying the principles of psychology and other social sciences.

"Their theory," Karen explained, "was that human interaction with computers is fundamentally social. A classic example is how people will often be more polite with one another in social situations. So if I'm saying to you, 'How am I doing?' you'd be more likely to say, 'Oh, great job!' But behind my back you'd be more honest."

Nass and Reeves set out to prove that the same phenomenon exists with human/computer interaction. So in one case, a computer that was tutoring a user asked the user how effective its tutoring was. In another case, they had a second computer ask the user how the first computer's tutoring was. People were always more polite when asked by the tutoring computer and more honest with the second one.

The presentation was a breakthrough for Karen. She realized their software had to obey the rules of social interaction.

With new prototypes, they began demonstrations across the company to gather broader support. They ran into skeptics. The problems, of course, were not only the cute characters but their own credibility. Their expertise was still in question.

Their persuasion strategy took several directions at this point. One thrust was to illustrate the dilemmas of today's software for the organization at large, as they had done for Gates. To do this, they presented customer research in the form of case examples and actual interview videos. A second step was to get Microsoft audiences to empathize with customers by having them share experiences of family or friends who were confused by computers. The third approach was to frame BOB as a necessary first step in a longer evolutionary process; upcoming technologies, they said, would soon dramatically enhance their software's less sophisticated features. "With skeptics—people put off by the cuteness of the characters—we'd talk about the future," Karen said. "We'd tell how we could use bitmaps to make our characters more photorealistic."

Along the way, they learned that exaggerating benefits and

playing only to the positives of BOB was not an effective persuasion approach. Since they lacked high levels of perceived expertise, such actions tended only to diminish their credibility. They found a balanced approach more successful.

"When we were with Bill Gates we wouldn't go in and pretend we had all the answers. We'd say, 'Here's what we know, this is what we know is really great. Here are the problems we have and what we're worried about,' " Karen said.

They used the prototypes to convince those who could not see their vision. When a staff member criticized an aspect of their design, they'd simply design a new prototype to address that criticism.

To compensate for their own lack of expertise they brought in Bryon Reeves and Clifford Nass on their project.

> We used Cliff and Bryon to help people understand it. We had a social-interface meeting where we invited everyone at the company, and we had Cliff and Bryon do the majority of the presentation because their credibility was high. They explained why the social interface is a viable concept, why it works, why humans are oriented toward social interaction. They validated the power of the social interface through a rigorous methodology. They also really believe deeply in the concepts behind BOB, and they see it as the first direct example of their theory put to test. They can just look at it and give you a hundred pieces of feedback on why it works based on their research. That is incredibly powerful.

Karen and Barry arranged another such meeting, this one between Bill Gates and Nass and Reeves. At that meeting, they presented the overall status of the project and an updated product demonstration. They had Nass explain his theory. This was a critical moment: "He [Gates] saw what the power of this whole concept was," Karen said. "It was a great meeting. It really helped frame for him what we were trying to do." ("Framing" is the process of describing a proposal so that it maximizes audience impact. The next chapter tells how to frame effectively.)

In addition, she laid out for Gates a vision of where technology would lead programs like BOB over the next five to ten years. It put BOB into perspective as a critical first step toward a software revolution. Soon Gates authorized a full thirty-five-person team, and in January of 1995, five years after Karen began, BOB was launched.

A year after its release, sales estimates put BOB at shy of 300,000 units. Not bad, but not a phenomenal success. Users apparently liked the approach but wanted more sophisticated characters for guides. Soon to come, a "secretary in a box" named Marilyn, whose image was adapted from a 1920's French artwork of an attractive young woman.[9] As Karen argued, BOB is only the first step.

Here are the critical lessons of the BOB example:

1. Lacking expertise, Karen found powerful substitutes for it.
2. Though her strong relationships in the company weren't enough to get her immediate support and resources, they did get her hearings for her ideas.

Strong Expertise and Weak Relationships

There are times when our expertise may be high, but because of a weak relational dimension we still face credibility problems. The ideal solution is to find someone else who is seen as having a strong relational position with our colleagues and to have them do the persuading on our behalf. That may mean that they present our positions for us, perhaps even taking the credit.

Guus Copeland, the manager of a successful radio station, had a client who spent some $48,000 a year in advertising for his retail operations. Guus believed that with a new $10,000 radio promotional campaign, he could improve his client's sales. He knew, however, that the $10,000 would be hard to get; the client had just ended a year with poor profits.

The decision on the increase in the promotional budget would be made jointly by three people—the company president, his executive assistant, and the manager of the company's largest store.

Each had a different personality and different objectives. The store manager, a flamboyant type, had been pleased with the radio station's campaigns and believed in the power of advertising. The executive assistant, a more cautious, detail-oriented fellow, would be concerned about the increased costs of a new campaign and whether the additional advertising would actually generate new revenues. The president was a Clint Eastwood character—cool, detached. He was very concerned about the bottom line and had a mixed opinion on advertising's effectiveness.

Guus carefully assessed his situation. All three men, he felt, would see him as skilled in devising ad campaigns, so when it came to expertise he was in a good position. The problem would be on the relationship dimension. He had a well-developed relationship with the store manager but no real ties to the other two. They would question his motives, seeing his proposal largely as a self-serving attempt to increase his radio station's revenues. Guus decided that if he tried to sell his idea himself, the president and his assistant would veto it.

Guus felt that, tactically, it would be smart to start his persuasion with the store manager, the only one of the three who believed in advertising and with whom he had a strong relationship. So he met separately with him to discuss the new campaign. He pitched him a campaign that used gaming elements borrowed from *The Price Is Right* television show to promote the company's retail outlets. The store manager reacted enthusiastically and pledged his support. With this manager's backing in place, Guus then set up the official meeting with all three decision makers.

The day of the meeting, Guus had some luck. Word was received that the president had been delayed and would be fifteen minutes late. Guus wasted no time. He began the meeting without him, focusing on the executive assistant.

Soon after he began, the store manager, whose enthusiasm had only grown since his meeting with Guus, jumped in to lay out his own arguments for the radio campaign. It was just what Guus thought might happen. So he kept his mouth shut and let the store manager assume the role of persuader. In a short time the executive assistant, who had great trust in the store manager, endorsed the campaign.

At that moment, the president arrived. Guus knew that the

president respected both the store manager and his executive assistant. So rather than intervene, Guus let those two do the pitch to the president. The president realized that, since his two key staff were already convinced by the merits of the budget increase, the need for further debate was limited. After a few minutes of discussion he announced the increase was approved.

Persuasion in this case was by proxy. Guus allowed others—who were seen as more credible and trustworthy on the relationship dimension—to do the persuading for him.

We must be careful, however, about enlisting others to supply the relationship dimension for us. Sometimes it can backfire. For one thing, we want to be sure our stand-in sees eye-to-eye with us on the issue at hand and can be an effective persuader himself.

There is another danger involved in borrowing relationship strength. Some persuaders try to shore up their credibility, for example, by drawing upon their relationship with a more powerful person in the organization. They'll come to you and say, "The president asked me to urge you to endorse this initiative."

Over and over again in research interviews, managers revealed to me that this approach, far from persuading them, often had the opposite effect: It undermined the credibility of the persuader. They felt that those who used this tactic hadn't the courage to speak for themselves; they were perceived as lacking conviction in what they were pushing. "It's weak," one manager told me. "You're weak as an individual if you have to drop names to get what you want. It's a real turnoff." Another said, "It probably would have worked twenty years ago. I could have said to someone, 'I work for so and so, vice president of global banking, and he would like it done this way.' It might have worked then, but not today. Now people resent it. They want to understand the logic: 'Help me understand why it should be done this way.' "

Exceptions, the managers said, were circumstances where people should be informed there might be serious political ramifications for failing to support a certain initiative backed by powerful people who are outside the immediate persuasion situation. In general, support from powerful outsiders can help us only if we ourselves and our position are already credible.

• • •

Think of the process of persuasion from the point of view of the person you're trying to persuade. For that person, making a decision on your proposal is like deciding which movie to go to.

He sees a newspaper ad for a new film and wonders whether or not to attend. The choice involves a measure of risk for him; two hours of a bad movie can feel like an eternity. So he needs all the information and convincing he can get.

He scans the ad for the names of the actors in the film and for the name of the director. He reads the list of excerpts from the reviews the film has received. He's learned from experience that some reviewers are quite credible and that some directors and stars almost always do a good job. Is it a Spielberg film? Is Tom Cruise in it, or Tommy Lee Jones?

What if the director is new and the stars hit-and-miss? He grows a bit anxious, takes a harder look at the reviews, and asks friends he knows who have seen the film. In the end he makes his choice.

In going to the movies, as in the world of business, it is judgments on credibility and reputation that open us to persuasion, that lead us into the theater. But when the titles come up on the screen, it's how we respond to the film itself, and not just to its reputation, that counts. We will make that judgment based on many factors, such as the quality of its plot and performances.

The next chapter will illustrate how framing persuasive arguments is equivalent to plotting a show. A good plot captures our attention and involves us. Certain techniques make the experience more appealing and captivating. In the persuasion process, effective framing achieves a similar goal. It attracts our colleagues' attention and makes our position more convincing.

Practice Session:
How to Build Credibility

So you're ready to persuade. You are fully convinced about a certain idea or initiative, and you're all set to present it to others.

Before you proceed, however, you'll want to do a mini-assessment of how credible you're likely to seem to your listeners. If the assessment highlights some weakness—in expertise or in relationships—you may need to lay some groundwork before you begin.

We'll start with expertise simply because it counts more than relationships do when we're trying to influence others.

Assessing Your Expertise

Think ahead to the persuasion session, and on a piece of paper list all the key people you'll have to persuade. Bill, Mary, Don, Mike—make sure you include them all.

Now take them one by one. Predict how each would rate you on the following characteristics. Use a 1 to 5 scale (1 means you'll be seen as "very weak" on that dimension, and 5 means that the person will see you as "very strong").

1. Your overall knowledge about the issue you are persuading
2. Your track record of accurate judgments on similar issues/initiatives in the past

Mike, for example, might see you as a "3" on overall knowledge and a "4" on track record. Now take the average of his two scores as his overall assessment of your expertise credibility.

Sit back and take a look at the numbers you've written down. If you end up with all 4s and 5s—and if you're correct in your assessments—then you are in a strong position on this credibility dimension. If you count mostly 1s, 2s, and 3s, then you'll have to find ways to compensate. We'll talk about those ways a bit later.

You may find that several of your colleagues rate you high while others rate you lower. It's this latter group that demands your attention before you even begin.

Now perform similar rankings for the relationship dimension of credibility. Go around your imaginary table of colleagues again and this time estimate the way they see you on these dimensions (1 implying "rarely" and 5 meaning "very often"):

1. You help one another out in mutually beneficial ways.
2. You are seen as having integrity.
3. You're emotionally in sync with them on issues like this one.

Again, take the average of each person's three scores as their assessment of your relationship credibility. High scores of 4s and 5s of course mean that you are strong on the relationship side of credibility. You won't need to make further relationship investments to get your points across.

If you are registering 1s, 2s, and 3s, though, you'll need to undertake some important relationship-building initiatives or find someone to advocate your position who has more strength on these dimensions than you.

If you're new to the group, then you may find you have low scores across the board. Don't take it personally. It just means you've got a big challenge ahead. The exception might be if everyone knows you were hired because you have special expertise. As long as the issue you are persuading is in that arena, you'll have strength on the expertise side and can focus on the relational aspect.

The thing about assessments like these is that they're only as accurate as our own self-perception. If you overestimate on the positive side, you'll be caught off guard when persuading. If you're an optimist, you'll tend toward overrating the appeal of your ideas. Pessimists tend to be much more realistic.

Assessing Your Assessments

What you need is a way to test out your assessments. The best way, if practical for you, is to go to a good friend at work, someone you can trust to keep a confidence and tell you the truth. Talk a bit about your interest in effective persuasion. (You can even tell him about this book, if you like.) Ask him if he'd be willing to go around that same imaginary table, just as you did, and estimate how those key colleagues rate you on expertise and relationships.

Emphasize your need for frankness in his assessments. You don't want compliments, you want candor.

Here's a refinement. If your colleague seems actively interested in this process, suggest that instead of a one-way evaluation, the two of you could make it a mutual effort: I'll assess for you if you assess for me. Maybe the arrangement could be expanded to colleagues in your lunch gang or car pool.

Choose these confidants carefully. Some people might find it odd that you're asking them whether so-and-so will see you as an expert. Afterward, they might ask themselves, "Why is Sallie asking these questions? Why the self-doubt?" Stay away from anyone who might misinterpret your motives. Also, avoid people so timid or so political that they'd never give you a lousy rating to your face.

If, however, you find the right person or people, you might want to make these assessments on an ongoing basis. That way, as you develop confidence in each other's judgment and discretion, you'll get more accurate, franker evaluations. Best of all, your network will develop a heightened awareness of the key factors that make for effective persuasion.

If your confidant's rankings are significantly lower than your own, err on the side of caution. Take a few extra steps before starting your persuasion. For example, if you are rated low on the expertise side, you'll need to find creative ways to build up perceptions of your expertise. Ask yourself: "What are the best proofs that I could present of my expertise?" You might circulate documents that you've written on the subject. Or, in informal settings with the colleagues thought to rate you low, you might discuss similar initiatives you have undertaken. Or you might cite outside consumer research studies you've conducted. I'll talk more about this a bit later.

Before you meet informally with one of these key people you'll be wanting to persuade, prep carefully. Make sure you can really demonstrate knowledge about your subject. Make a brief list of what each individual would expect to hear from a real expert. Try to find ways of supplying equivalents.

Ramon, your colleague in manufacturing, is going to want to know how this new product will impact his operations. How's it been engineered for production? Wendy, your colleague in marketing, will want to know how the product will sell to her range of customers. Tailor the type of knowledge you present to each.

How to Build Up Perceptions of Expertise

You have three general options on expertise. (You can use all three at once.)

Option One is to *find experts* who can speak on your behalf, just as Karen Fries and Barry Linnett of Microsoft did. Think for a moment about individuals in your company who know your issue well, who would be seen as real experts on it, and who happily support your position. Think about outsiders as well—consultants or a local professor or an engineer friend. Invite these individuals to present to the group. Beforehand, carefully go over your own ideas with them to ensure that you're both on the same wavelength.

Option Two is to *circulate supporting evidence*. You'll want to find articles or consultants' reports or company studies that prove your point yet are seen as objective sources. My advice is to gather as many of these as you can. You may want to do an Internet search as well. Then judiciously sort through what you have. Select only the material that clearly and powerfully supports your position. Avoid the tendency to send out everything; if you do they'll read little of it. Better to find three or four key articles or short reports that do the job.

Two characteristics you'll want to look for in this material:

1. Who's the source? The more credible the source in the eyes of your colleagues, the more they will pay attention. So an article in the *National Enquirer* is not likely to have the impact of a study conducted by the nationally ranked consulting company McKinsey. An article written in the *Harvard Business Review* by an acclaimed professor of marketing might just be perfect for persuading Andrea, the senior marketing manager on the team. A paper from the American Society of Engineers might do the trick for Evan, the production coordinator. The key is to find articles or reports that cite evidence from leading companies or universities or highly respected individuals. These are powerful stand-ins for your expertise.
2. The best material will describe opposing viewpoints and then carefully explain why these approaches will not work as effectively. Essentially, you're letting these sources address the counterarguments that your colleagues might have.

Use these criteria to bring your stack down to only a handful. These are the ones to circulate.

Option Three is to *launch a pilot or develop a prototype* of your idea, again, as Karen and Barry did at Microsoft. Ask yourself what you could do that would, in a small way, parallel what you are proposing to your colleagues. If this goes well, then use this "mini-success" as one proof of your position.

How to Build Up Relationship Strength

If the relationship dimension is our weak spot, we have a choice. We can either attempt to build up our relationships with the key individuals or we can try to find substitutes. It all depends on how much time we have.

If you have the time, meet informally with the colleagues you'll be trying to persuade. Without giving them your actual position, get their reactions to a wide array of perspectives on the initiative you'll be proposing or the issue you'll be arguing. Get them to talk about their worries and their hopes. If you can help out or support a project of their own, then do so.

But you may not have time for that. In which case, sit down for a moment. Make a list of anyone you know to have strong relationships with the key people you'll be persuading. If you're fortunate you'll find one or two people. Ideally, they will be either respected department outsiders or one of your colleagues already involved in the issue. You're looking for someone who shares your perspective on the issue but has a stronger relationship with the other players than you. They also need to be a confidant, someone you can trust.

Approach them. Would they be willing to be the point person to propose and argue the issue?

Case in Point:
How Aaron Built Credibility

Aaron is trying to get his fellow vice presidents to reengineer the counter service at his company's chain of fast-food restaurants. He's the VP of sales, and he knows from customer surveys that the speed of service has slipped since the company introduced a new meal line that has been enormously popular. As he scans his imaginary table with the peers he must persuade seated around it, he begins an assessment.

He starts with the dimension of expertise and begins with Ray. He's pretty sure Ray will rank him a 2 on expertise. Ray is VP of operations and is the real expert on restaurant layouts. Three major redesigns have occurred under him in the last dozen years. The last one was a year and a half ago. So he'll be hesitant to launch another one.

On the other hand, Aaron figures that Jason, VP of marketing, will rank him a 4 on expertise. Jason and Aaron often visit company restaurants together and talk frequently about the layouts. He'll feel that Aaron has a real hands-on understanding of layouts.

Cindy, the VP of finance, will give Aaron a 2. She'll figure that Aaron does not fully understand the cost of redesigning a layout and will underestimate the cost of changing the service design.

Chet, the company president, Aaron thinks, will likely give him a 2.5 for expertise. He and Aaron don't see much of each other outside of senior team meetings, so he'll think that Aaron just doesn't have Ray's depth.

As Aaron looks down his column of rankings, he sees he'll clearly have to do some preparatory work with Ray, Cindy, and Chet.

Now for relationships. As Aaron lists his rankings in the relationship column, he realizes he has a great deal of strength in this area. He's been at the company for ten years and has strong ties to just about all the key players. For example, he socializes regularly with everyone except Chet.

He puts a 5 under Ray. Last year, he supported Ray in an operations initiative that made life more difficult for Aaron's group but is now paying great dividends for company profitability. Ray's idea really ensured that the company could weather the "value-meal" era. Ray will remember that Aaron already put the company first, over his own area, and won't have any trouble believing that, with this proposal of Aaron's, he's doing it again.

He figures Cindy for a 4. He's been very cooperative and speedy with implementing her new financial reporting systems. And she knows that he cares about costs, which is her primary concern.

As for Jason, he and Aaron see eye-to-eye on just about every company matter. They're golfing buddies and confidants. He can tell Jason almost anything, and vice versa. So Jason rates a 5.

Aaron marks a 3 next to Chet's name. Chet will feel that Aaron has been a real team player and someone who will candidly speak his mind. Two years ago, however, Aaron didn't see eye-to-eye with Chet on a strategy initiative. Chet was surprised by Aaron's perspective on the issue. Also, though their relationship is almost always cordial, Aaron has never really responded to Chet's cool demeanor, and Chet probably senses that.

In sum, Aaron has a strong relationship dimension, but he may need to pay a bit more attention to Chet.

Aaron approaches his confidant, Jason. He shows him his assessments and asks if they seem realistic. Jason is impressed that Aaron is taking the issue so seriously. As he scans the numbers, they look realistic to him, except for the assessment of Chet. Jason feels Aaron is being too tough on that rating. Jason knows Chet quite well, and they've often discussed how sharp Aaron is. Jason ups Aaron's estimates of Chet's scores to 4s on both the expertise and relationship dimensions.

Having completed his assessments, Aaron decides that before he proposes anything he first needs to meet with Chet and Cindy. At lunch with each, he casually raises the matter of the service problems caused by the new meal lineup. He doesn't want to focus their attention immediately on the issue of restaurant layouts; he keeps the discussion open-ended.

Chet and Cindy raise a number of factors, many of them similar. Among them is the possible layout problem. Cindy thinks it's just a temporary problem that will vanish as employees adapt to the pace or as the appeal of a new product gradually fades with time. Chet is cautious, saying that they need another month before the company can tell more accurately whether the sales curve is really on a longer-term uptake thanks to the new meals.

Hearing this, Aaron decides to wait before raising the issue. He knows that Chet will have considerable influence on the others. If he thinks the group needs to wait one more month to check sales, Aaron will wait.

A month passes. Sales continue on their upward trend. From reports, service levels are showing further slippage. Aaron is now ready to move. In the group's monthly meeting, he highlights the service slippage and hands out copies of the results of focus group interviews conducted by marketing; they confirm that customers are sensing that service is slowing down. (Two days before the meeting, Aaron sent every team member a *Harvard Business Review* article on why companies need to catch service problems early.)

Now he lists for the group all the possible causes of the problem. Somewhere in the middle of his list he quietly mentions layouts—and keeps going. He doesn't want to draw too much attention to the issue, just to test reactions.

Both Jason and Chet zero in on the subject of restaurant layouts. After some debate, Aaron proposes that they employ a local consulting group to investigate the layout issue. This would be a lower-cost, low-risk way to verify the problem. Ray agrees. The consultants' report will later confirm the problem as a layout issue.

Working with Ray, Cindy, Jason, and Chet, Aaron produces a plan that revamps the restaurant's kitchen designs at a relatively low cost. The project is a success, with service levels exceeding past highs.

Table 1
Credibility Tactic Grid

	Weak	Strong
Strong	Investigate colleagues' concerns about issues beforehand. Network beforehand to ensure support. Involve others who have stronger relationships to persuade your case.	Persuade directly using techniques of framing, compelling positions/ evidence, and emotional connection.
Weak	Network beforehand to ensure support. Involve others who have stronger relationships and expertise to persuade on your behalf. Involve outside experts and credible references that validate your position. Seek early proofs/ successes/prototypes of your position beforehand as confirming evidence.	Involve outside experts to validate. Bring in externally validated evidence (e.g., market research, consultants' reports). Create pilots/prototypes/ mini-successes that prove your position.

Your Expertise Reputation

Weak   Strong
Your Relationship Reputation

4
Searching for Shared Ground

Even if your relationships are terrific and your expertise is spectacular, that doesn't mean you've got it made. You still have to structure your arguments carefully. You still have to choose your perspectives, evidence, and data in ways that will make your position attractive to others.

In earlier chapters we encountered managers who thought that to be persuasive, all they had to do was state their position up front followed by a few supporting arguments—the wham-bam school of persuasion. We saw that in most of those cases no one but the persuader was persuaded.

To be truly effective at persuasion, we have to think strategically about our position. We have to align it to address colleagues' concerns. A highly effective persuader I met during my research once said to me: "The most valuable lesson I've learned about persuasion is that there's just as much strategy in how you *present* your position as in the plan or idea itself. In fact, I'd say the strategy of presentation is the more critical."

The secret is to shape our position and its supporting arguments so that our colleagues feel our plan will satisfy their concerns and bring them the benefits they hope for. As we've noted several times, it's not just a matter of how we perceive these concerns and benefits; it's also a question of how our colleagues perceive them.

The Notion of Framing

Any professional photographer knows the importance of composing his photos effectively. He zooms in on an image or steps back to get a broader perspective or turns the lens to get an angled view. Photographing the same object, he can frame the shot differently and get strikingly different results in terms of mood and impact.

It's the same with framing ideas and arguments. Perhaps no other single technique of effective persuasion has as much effect as the way we frame what we are proposing.

Lee Iacocca, for example, was a master at framing issues so that they were highly persuasive. In his now famous turnaround of Chrysler, he framed the need for a government bailout around a "reality," as he termed it, that to do otherwise would be jeopardizing the American free enterprise system:

> We were asking [the government]: Would this country really be better off if Chrysler folded and the nation's unemployment rate went up another half of one percent overnight? Would free enterprise really be saved if Chrysler failed and tens of thousands of jobs were lost to the Japanese? Would our free-market system really be more competitive without the million-plus cars and trucks that Chrysler builds and sells each year?. . . . We explained [to the government] that we're really an amalgam of little guys, we're an assembly company. We have eleven thousand suppliers and four thousand dealers. Almost all of these people are small businessmen—not fat cats. We need a helping hand—not a handout.[1]

Now what was the reality of the actual situation? Well, Chrysler was indeed in danger of going bankrupt. It certainly would have been a major bankruptcy. But would Chrysler's demise really have jeopardized the American free enterprise system? No, not likely. There would have been economic repercussions, but would competition really have been lessened in a marketplace of more than twenty international automobile manufacturers? Again, not likely.

For Iacocca, however, the situation was desperate. To survive, Chrysler somehow had to obtain a very large amount of financing. Iacocca could have framed arguments to Congress projecting attractive financial returns on any government financing, but these would not have had the national appeal needed to get congressional approval. He could have accurately said: "Look, the company is in a dire financial situation, and we are going to lose thousands of jobs. Please help us." But this would not have been as compelling as linking Chrysler to thousands of small businesses throughout America and to the increased threat of Japanese domination of a traditional American industry. He very effectively framed the issue as a problem threatening the core of the American free enterprise system. In the end, this frame was effective. Chrysler got the bailout.

The frames we choose profoundly impact how people respond to our persuasion. The way we frame an opportunity, for example, influences expectations. What if I gave you the choice between a gambling opportunity that offered an 85 percent chance to win $1,000 and the alternative of getting $800 for certain? Most people would choose the sure outcome over the gamble—even though mathematically the gamble is a better choice. (It has a higher return and an 85 percent chance of occurring.) Now if I switch the game so you'd choose between an 85 percent chance of losing $1,000 or a sure loss of $800, which would you take? Most people prefer the gamble even though statistically it is the less attractive of the options.[2] They're influenced by the way the proposition is framed.

In one research study, participants were told of a project having an 80 percent chance of success and of another project having a 20 percent chance of failure and then were asked to choose one. Inevitably, they chose the former, yet both outcomes are the same. These are just a few simple examples of how framing shifts our subjective perspectives.

A friend of mine and professor at McGill University, Frances Westley, recently studied the achievement of a remarkable leader, Dr. Balfort Mount.[3] In the 1980s Dr. Mount pioneered in the field of palliative care. Palliative care is the humane treatment of terminally ill patients by coordinated teams of hospital staff; both the patient and his family are treated as a unit. The aim is to minister not just to his physical needs but to his social, psychological, and spiritual needs as well.

Setting up the first such program was an enormous challenge. At that time no hospital in North America offered in-house palliative care. Terminally ill patients were traditionally treated by specialists rather than by integrated teams of doctors and nurses. So Mount's system required a radical mindshift on the part of the staff.

Early in his quest, he identified the people he had to persuade. "I looked around and realized there were two or three people who had to be convinced," he said, "because they controlled the outcomes. I had to slowly work with them."[4] These three staff members, the "change brokers" in this situation, were the chief of surgery, the head of nursing, and the chief of professional services. His core message to each would be essentially the same: Let's radically reorganize the process of patient care. But with each he framed that message so that it spoke to his unique concerns, stressing the ways palliative care would assist him with *his own personal agenda*.

When he talked to the head of nursing, for example, he emphasized that the treatment team members would all be equal—a departure from the traditional hospital care model of doctor-dominated teams. She liked that; it would give nurses prestige equal to doctors'. Mount also knew that the chief of professional services was a deeply religious man. Mount persuaded him by underlining the whole-patient approach and the fact that spiritual needs would be included in the care giving. As for the chief of surgery, he was a strong advocate of innovation; with him, Mount described the research aspects of the palliative care experiment.

When he spoke to the hospital's doctors he connected his approach to the medical profession's ideals of scientific rigor and professionalism. One doctor later explained:

> The secret of [Mount's] success was that he hooked
> into that something spiritual, something emotional,

something idealistic, that is in most doctors. Many were suspicious, but Mount packaged it in a way that was scientifically and intellectually acceptable. There are a lot of people who get you crying but in the cold light of day you say: "How can I support this?". . . . Mount was able to identify the "hooks" and use them to link key people to his larger purposes.[5]

At the core of effective framing is this search for shared ground and shared advantage with those whom we are attempting to persuade. Framing tends to fail when it reflects only our own perspective. (Unless, as it happens, our perspective is, at the start, a widely shared one. If it is, there is little need for persuasion.)

Returning for a moment to the analogy of a camera, we can think of our own perspective on an issue as one lens angle. Our audience may or may not find the picture from that angle as attractive as we do. What we have to do is position the lens so that the view appeals to our audience and to ourselves. In some cases, this may mean searching for a wider angle, so that the picture includes more—the way Iacocca linked Chrysler and American free enterprise. Or you may have to frame tighter and more specifically, as Mount did with each of his key change agents.

Before attempting to persuade, the best persuaders I've encountered study the issues that matter to their audiences. In brief office chats or in telephone calls or in meetings, they collect essential information. They seek out sources who can inform them about their audience's concerns and hopes. They are very good at listening. They ask themselves questions like those listed further along in this chapter. They test their ideas with trusted confidants. They may ask questions of the people they will later try to persuade.

As they go through this process, they rethink the arguments, evidence, and perspectives they will present. Sometimes the process causes them to alter or compromise their plans before the actual persuasion, to ensure ultimate acceptance. Through this thoughtful, inquisitive approach they develop frames that work.

The Framing Triad

Truly effective framing depends on your ability to create three kinds of positions:

1. positions based around *goals and rewards* to be shared by our audience;
2. positions incorporating *values and beliefs* shared by our audience;
3. positions delivered in a *language* shared by our audience.

Each kind assures our colleagues that we're not prisoners of our own point of view.

Table 1
The Framing Triad

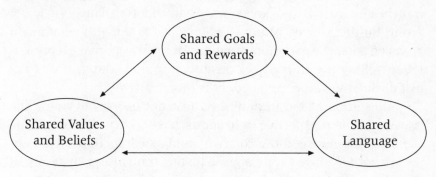

The Appeal to Shared Goals and Rewards

I've said this many times in these pages already, I know, but it's so important I'll say it again: You'll persuade your coworkers to your position only if they feel it contains rewards for themselves.[6] For this reason, you must understand their needs. People's needs, of course, differ. An appeal to a group of bond traders must be framed quite differently from an appeal to a group of environmentalists. So step one is to frame your position around advantages that are attractive to the people you're addressing.

If you don't have a firm grasp of their perspective, there is always the chance that you'll guess wrong about what will appeal

to them. You mustn't be fooled by what you *think* will be advantageous for your colleagues. You've got to know for sure.

For example, Monica Ruffo, an account executive at a Canadian advertising firm, was up against a difficult persuasion situation, but she found goals and rewards with such strongly shared
appeal that she quickly won her audience over. Her client, a fast-
food restaurant chain, was instituting a "value campaign" in Canada; certain menu items such as a Coke, fries, and a burger were
to be bundled and offered under a single promotional price. This
value campaign meant a new pricing strategy—lower prices. The
people at headquarters knew that the company was seen as having
higher prices than its competitors, and they were anxious to overcome this market perception.

The franchisees, however, did not fully grasp the possible
long-term competitive benefits of this pricing strategy. They were
concerned about the short-term impact that the new strategy
would have on their profit margins. Sales were still strong, and the
franchisees feared that lower prices would translate into lower
profits for themselves. Monica's agency was faced with what might
be called a hairy persuasion situation: Its job was to make a presentation selling the franchisees on lowering their outlet prices not
just during the value campaign but "forever."

One thing Monica knew she must not do was to frame the
issue from the perspective of headquarters—charts demonstrating
the price gap between the company and its competition. That approach would have scant appeal to the franchisees in terms of
shared rewards. No, what they were concerned about was protecting
store profits. She knew she'd have to build her presentation with
this at the center of the frame.

In her presentation to the several hundred franchisees she
ducked the controversial matter of lowering pricing to meet the
competition and began with the greatest concern for the franchisees—their stores' profitability. The meal pricing scheme, she said,
would actually improve franchisees' profits. She told about a small
market test in Tennessee. There a pilot project had demonstrated
that under the new "whole meal" pricing scheme the sales of
french fries and drinks had actually increased. That impressed the
franchisees: Fries and drinks were the two most profitable products
on the menu.

Her second argument to her Canadian audience was that the company already had medium-size meal packages in 80 percent of its U.S. outlets. Within this one category, franchisees' sales of fries and drinks had jumped 26 percent. It was powerful evidence that value meals boosted sales of high-profit items.

Finally, Monica cited research described in a recent article in *Harvard Business Review*. It showed that when customers of an establishment raised by 10 percent their estimate of the value they got, then the establishment's sales rose by 1 percent. Given that the fast-food company's low-cost value meals were expected to increase value perception by 100 percent, Monica said, then franchisees' sales could be expected to increase by some 10 percent. What's more, she added, a big portion of those sales would be in profitable fries and drinks.

She ended her presentation by reading a memo written years before by the founder of the organization. It was a very moving letter. It extolled the values of the company and stressed the importance of franchisees to the corporation. It also underlined the importance of the company's positioning as the low-price player in its industry. This, he said, was what the company did best and why it was the consistent winner in the industry.

Monica could tell that by closing with the letter, she'd make sure the presentation would end on a value-laden, emotional peak, one that made the franchisees forget any doubts they might have had. She was right. As she finished, the franchisees rose and applauded loudly. Later that day they voted unanimously to support the company's new meal-pricing plan.

Monica had very skillfully framed the long-term pricing change in a manner that had meaning to her audience.

As you begin to think about how to frame your own position for an upcoming persuasion situation, you can start by asking yourself the following questions:

1. What aspects of my idea will have significant appeal to my colleagues? What other advantages might my colleagues be looking for? How can I incorporate these?
2. How can I demonstrate to them in terms of *expected outcomes* that I share their goals and that there will be a shared reward?

3. If shared goals and rewards are not apparent, how can I adapt my position so that it will clearly have these attractions?

Answering these questions may lead you to the conclusion that you've got to make some compromises. You can't sell others on a solution that offers them little or nothing. Begin identifying the areas where by adapting your position you can broaden its appeal.

In short, tie your initiative to tangible benefits for all involved. A plant manager trying to persuade the company's chief financial officer to okay the purchase of a new but costly piece of equipment should tie that purchase to something the officer is really interested in. For example, he might show how it will lead to more accurate cost information for finance.

The Appeal to Shared Values and Beliefs

An effective frame usually incorporates values and beliefs that are widely held by an audience.[7] (See Table 2 on page 96 for a list of basic American values.) Their presence adds strength to the appeal. In the earlier example, Iacocca employed the deeply held American values of free enterprise and entrepreneurship to buttress his pitch for a bailout of his company. Monica used the fast-food company values the same way in her appeal to its franchisees.

Business people have a lot to learn from politicians about the use of shared values and beliefs in persuasion. John F. Kennedy, for example, was a master at it. In the early 1960s a group of steel manufacturers joined to raise their prices. Kennedy feared that other industries would do likewise, fueling inflation. He wanted those prices lowered, so after preliminary discussions with the steel executives failed, he appeared on national television to apply public pressure.

Kennedy cleverly associated steel prices to the nation's deepest values and beliefs. Knowing how hard it would be to arouse the public about steel prices in themselves, he instead framed the steel controversy in terms of one of the nation's most emotionally charged values—its security:

In this serious hour in our nation's history, when we are confronted with grave crises in Berlin and Southeast Asia, when we are devoting our energies to our economic recovery and stability, when we are asking reservists to leave their homes and families for months on end and servicemen to risk their lives in Vietnam, and asking union members to hold down their wage requests; at a time when restraint and sacrifice are being asked of every citizen, the American people will find it hard as I do to accept a situation in which a tiny handful of steel executives whose pursuit of private power and profit exceeds their sense of public responsibility can show such utter contempt for the interests of 185 million Americans.

If this rise in the cost of steel is initiated by other industries instead of rendered, it would increase the cost of homes, autos, appliances, and most other items. It would increase the cost of machinery and tools to every American businessman and farmer. It would seriously handicap our efforts to prevent an inflationary spiral from eating up the pensions of our older citizens. It would add, Secretary McNamara informed me this morning, an estimated one billion dollars to the cost of our defenses at a time when every dollar is needed for national security and other purposes.

It would make it more difficult for American goods to compete in foreign markets, more difficult to withstand competition from foreign imports, and thus more difficult to improve our balance of payments position and stem the flow of gold. And it is necessary to stem it for our national security if we're going to pay for our security commitments abroad. And it would surely handicap our effort to induce other industries and unions to adopt responsible price and wage policies. The facts of the matter are that there is no justification for an increase in steel prices.

What Kennedy did so cleverly was to link the action of the steel executives to a long list of threatening outcomes. He started

with the sacrifices that many American citizens were already making and, by implication, how greedy the steel executives must have
been. Then he connected the price hikes to everyday lives, the
health of the economy, and to national security.

Now he could have framed the price increases so that the
thrust was inflation fears. But if he'd done that, he couldn't have
spurred the public condemnation of the steel executives that he'd
wanted. Instead, he appealed to national values. It worked. The
public was outraged and in the end the steel executives lowered
their prices.

Kennedy was using the values-and-beliefs approach to persuade some people *not* to take a certain action, but managers can
use it to deepen colleagues' commitment, just as Monica did in the
fast-food example. One business leader who uses values extensively is Mary Kay Ash, founder of Mary Kay Cosmetics. At her
annual sales conventions, she uses stories to convey the critical
values that she believes are necessary for success at Mary Kay
Cosmetics. Her challenge is always the same: to build a force of
motivated salespeople who can survive the rigors of selling cosmetics. Her comments from this speech show how she does it:

> Back in the days of the Roman Empire the legions of
> the emperor conquered the known world. These soldiers
> moved from nation to nation bringing into subjection
> people from the coasts of Spain to the borders of India.
> There was, however, one band of people the Romans
> never conquered. These people were the followers of the
> great teacher from Bethlehem.
>
> Historians have long since discovered that one of
> the reasons for the sturdiness of this fold was their habit
> of meeting together weekly. They shared their difficulties
> and then stood side by side. Does this remind you of
> something? The way we stand side by side and share our
> knowledge as well as our difficulties with each other at
> our weekly unit meetings.
>
> I have so often observed when a director or unit
> member is confronted with a personal problem that the
> unit stands together in helping that sister in distress.

What a wonderful circle of friendships we have. Perhaps it's one of the greatest fringe benefits of our company, in making so many friends, beginning with our customers and going on through our association with our unit members.

The shared value she is tapping into is Christianity. She knew that her sales people held the Christian model in high regard, and that they would identify with the story of a brave group of people in dire circumstances (door-to-door selling is no picnic). By standing together and supporting one another, she points out, they not only survived but flowered into one of the world's great religions. The message for Mary Kay's salespeople is plain to each of them: Stand together and support one another, and you'll not only weather the ups and downs of selling but you will go forth to some form of greatness in your own life.

Then Mary Kay deals with her listeners' worst problem—getting doors slammed in their faces, getting hung up on when they phone, getting turned down when they ask for an order. She knows of course that the vast majority of her sales force will experience failure on an almost daily basis. So she attempts to give them a new mindset about failure, one that will encourage them to persist despite setbacks:

> And finally, . . . growth comes from learning how to turn failure into success. It was Keats who said, "Failure is, in a sense, the highway to success in as much as every discovery of what is false leads us to seek earnestly for that which is true, and every fresh experience points out some form of error which we shall afterwards carefully avoid."
>
> That quotation has stood the test of time. You've often heard me say that we fail forward to success. In the founding days of our company, when I took that legal pad and wrote down the problems I had experienced, and challenged myself to find solutions for them, I was seeking ways to turn failures into successes.
>
> The Mary Kay marketing plan which resulted was

formulated, in large part, on correcting errors that other companies, in my experience, had made.

Just as the wounded oyster mends itself with a pearl, so *we* can turn errors into pearls that make our lives and our company work.

In this case, Mary Kay draws upon the shared societal belief that learning is an essential part of growth. She takes failure, which is not normally considered a positive value, and transforms it into one: Failure is a necessary and positive experience on our way to success.

What we are doing when we incorporate shared values and beliefs into our persuasion is drawing on the power residing in the common concern, the common experience, the common destiny, the common aspiration. We're linking ourselves and our position to our colleagues on a profound emotional level. By going directly to the emotions, we can often bypass more rational critiques of our message.

The Appeal Through a Shared Language

The level and style of the language we use—whether elevated or colloquial or journalistic or scientific—is very important in persuasion. Language is the most significant means we have of establishing a connection with someone. Social scientists have long known this power of language to influence. "Sharing a language with other persons," said the scholar C. W. Morris, "provides the subtlest and most powerful of all tools for controlling the behavior of . . . other persons to one's advantage.[8]

Returning to the example of Dr. Mount and his ability to convince others of the importance of his vision of palliative care, we recall that one of his gifts was his ability to present his ideas in a language each of his audiences understood. As one staff doctor described it:

Mount took great care to speak the language of his audience at all times. Once they felt engaged into his excitement, they rationally could also say, "This makes sense," whether the person needed scientific language, political language, or spiritual language.

Using a shared language improves a frame's effectiveness because it creates a sense that the persuader is a peer with his colleagues, that he shares, at some level, in his audience's situation, that he is one of them. If it is a highly sophisticated group, then using their language tends to give you, in effect, similar standing.

The phenomenon is most powerfully apparent with executives communicating to the lowest levels of their organizations. An executive is expected to use an elevated style of language, so when he unexpectedly uses a few phrases of the colloquial language of the plant worker, it may create a special positive response—affection, admiration.[9] In one company I studied, a senior manager explained the charisma of his boss in terms of this quality:

> He would go into the plants and tour them, talk to the employees, say, "Hey, big guy, what's happening? How's it been going with you?" He'd drop his sophistication a few levels until the person he was talking to really felt relaxed. People really felt comfortable with him. They felt he understood them. He could relate and speak at their level. That was an important part of what attracted people to him.

But the use of the language of subordinates must be sincere and feel natural. If it appears contrived, it will produce the opposite effect.

Ross Perot, the founder of Electronic Data Systems, is a well-known example of an individual who can create a shared language with audiences of ordinary people. He does this through short, sharply phrased comments that employ everyday images. They have a folksy, punchy quality that makes Perot's ideas often appealing and understandable to the general populace. Here is a perfect example, from an appearance on *Larry King Live* in 1992, when Perot was contemplating a presidential campaign:

King: What about this system [of government that]
would keep someone like Perot away from wanting to
lead it?

Perot: It's a system that doesn't work. For example, right
now we have fundamental economic problems. We owe
$4 trillion that we admit to. . . . We are going to run
up a huge budget deficit this year "jump-starting the
economy."

   Now, let's just talk about jump-starting. I'm stalled
on the side of the highway. You come by and you say,
"Ross, what's the problem?" I say, "My battery's dead."
You jump-start me. With luck, I'll get to the filling station, right? What I really need is a fundamental fix for
the problem.

Masterfully Perot casts his argument in the commonplace language of his audience. He creates a dialogue between friends,
which enables him to pose a question to himself ("Ross, what is the
problem?"). The tone of the discussion is colloquial and intimate—
nothing like a typical public policy address. He makes use of an
analogy—jump-starting the dead car battery; it's an image totally
familiar to all of his listeners. He extends that homely analogy to a
national problem, the deficit.

   He doesn't use sophisticated economic jargon or go into detailed explanations, despite the fact that the problem is an enormously complex one. He's well aware that his audience, the
general public, is unfamiliar with the terminology of economists
and the intricacies of government budgets. He uses an exceed-
ingly simple and familiar comparison to persuade the audience
of the short-term nature and ultimate folly of the government's
solution.

   The use of expressions or terminology familiar to an audience
may achieve the same outcome as use of a shared language. One
chief executive I know, who heads a highly diversified conglomer-
ate, does some research before paying visits to his frontline employees. Inconspicuously he asks about the workplace terminology
current among them. His food processing plant may have just in-
stalled new equipment that processes quite differently from equip-

ment in the past. From his inquiries, the CEO is able to question staff knowledgeably about their reactions to the equipment, using the appropriate technical lingo. His employees are invariably impressed and open up to him as if he's one of their own. When this CEO needs to mobilize frontline employee support behind a proposal, he usually has little trouble getting it.

To make sure that the language you use is shared by your particular audiences, you need to ask yourself some questions:

1. Does the vocabulary you choose—the slang, the level of sophistication—match those of your listeners?
2. Will your terminology, the terms used by your listeners in their work—scientific, manufacturing, financial, etc.— sound knowledgeable and authentic to them?
3. Is the tone you choose, e.g., easy-going versus humorous versus serious, right for these listeners, this occasion?
4. Is the emotional level right: enthusiastic versus anxious versus confident?
5. Are you using analogies, metaphors, and images that are familiar to your audience and connect with their own experience of life?

The more accurately you can gauge your audience on these criteria and the more skillfully you can match your presentation to them, the better you'll be at the essential craft of framing.

Whether or not to use slang is the trickiest of all the choices. If you use slang that is unfamiliar to you or seems out of place given who you are (swear words, for example, if your usual style is never to use them), then your audience may see your language and yourself as contrived. So be careful.

The challenge is to continually remember that framing must be tailored to each and every audience. The framing of an initiative will necessarily have to change with each level and each function of our organization. One size will not fit everyone.

In the next section, we'll see why.

How One Manager Succeeded and Then Failed at Framing

I am going to illustrate framing in action with an example of one manager who used framing successfully to get buy-in at senior levels of his organization but then misframed the same initiative for more junior levels.

Charlie managed the process-engineering group of an aircraft turbine manufacturer. He and his team had been working on various redesigns of the work flow, especially the flow in turbine maintenance.

Normally, as turbines are being serviced, they travel in line across a long work floor. It's like an automobile line but without the continuous movement. At different points in that line, different checkups and repairs are performed. Over the course of the year, a work group will encounter a number of models of turbine. They might spend a few weeks on an engine from a Boeing 737, then shift to one from a DC-9, then repair one from a 727. Most of the engines, however, are made by the company itself—just different models.

Charlie and his group realized that this system, in which a mix of turbines comes down the line and the maintenance crew takes them as they come, was slow and expensive. In turbine maintenance, once you meet quality standards, speed and economy are what it's all about. Airlines want to get their engines back fast and want their bill to be low. A company that can satisfy the airlines in those two respects can put itself way ahead of the competition.

Charlie and his crew decided the answer was to simplify things. The ideal would be to have each line focus on a single turbine type. That way the crew on a line wouldn't have to switch equipment around every time a new type of turbine came along. The setup could remain the same, saving a lot of time, and each team would become highly expert in its particular engine, and therefore speedier. Charlie and his team convinced themselves that specialized lines were indeed the best solution.

At about this time, Charlie went off to Montreal to attend the program on managing change I was teaching at McGill University. In one session I stressed the importance of finding apt and memorable ways to convey ideas. Inspired, Charlie came up with cows. Yes, cows. He would use cows to explain his new maintenance plan to the senior executives of his company.

When he went for his audience with the company's president

and top managers, Charlie trotted out his cow analogy. The turbine maintenance operation, he said, was like a barn with one narrow door. Through that door came all the cows—the turbines—and the maintenance crew took them as they came: first a white cow, then a brown cow, then a black cow, then a tall one, then a short one. Charlie said the different kind of cows represented the different turbine types.

It wasn't a perfect analogy. I suppose, presumably, milking a brown cow is the same as milking a short cow. But the executives didn't mind. They enjoyed Charlie and his cows.

Charlie pressed on. What he and his team had realized, he said, was that there were big efficiencies and savings to be had if the farmer built a new door in the barn for each kind of cow. The managers got the point and a serious discussion followed.

Charlie's strength was not with his barnful-of-cows speech but with the wisdom of what he'd done earlier. At the Montreal program on managing change, he had learned that before persuasions like this one he should do lots of homework. So he scoped out the executive team, especially the president. A talk to the vice president of engineering, a good friend in the organization, revealed that the president's prime concern would be the project's contribution to the company profitability. Charlie, said the vice president, somehow had to show that his new system would improve company profitability in the short-run by lowering expenses.

At first this had Charlie stumped. His original focus was on efficiency. But efficiency alone would not win the president over. Charlie had wanted the company to put some money into installing the new system properly; now he knew that wouldn't fly. So he changed his proposal so it no longer required new investment, and he reframed it, this time as a profitability initiative. The president was persuaded.

This was when Charlie went wrong. Thinking he now had the project in the bag, Charlie went to his functional peers in the company and said, "The president has approved this new system. Now help us implement it." Not much happened. The other divisions of the company resisted the plan, and it languished.

Charlie would later learn why he'd failed. He'd framed the

project for the president, but he'd neglected to reframe it for each of his peers. He hadn't realized he'd have to make different types of compromises for each function. What he'd done so well at the executive level, he'd done poorly at the lower levels—levels that were critical to his project's success.

The lesson is not that you shouldn't count your cows before you've milked them. It's never safe to assume that the frame and the compromises we make to persuade one level of our organization are the same ones needed to persuade other levels. Each area has different concerns, and these have to be addressed.

For all its rural imagery, the story vividly documents the key lesson of this book: We live in an age where other functions determine the success or failure of our initiatives. We need to be persuasive at all levels.

Frames are one of our most powerful persuasion tools. But ultimately to succeed, they need to be supported by positions and evidence that are compelling. In the next chapter, we'll learn how to do this.

Practice Session: How to Find Common Ground

The first thing to do, when you create a frame for your presentation, is to put yourself into the minds of the people you need to persuade. Most persuaders never wander beyond their own minds. They fail to see that others might interpret their position quite differently. This set of exercises is meant to burst you out of the prison of your own head and beckon you into the heads of your colleagues.

Exercise One

Let's go back to the list of individuals that you drew up in the last chapter. Take the first name. Think hard about that person's job and the outlook that goes with it. As he listens to your argument, how will his functional background be influencing his perspective on it?

Let's say you're the information systems director, and you're trying to persuade your division to upgrade certain computer systems.

One of the vice presidents who'll be involved in the approval of funds for your project is the marketing VP.

Write his name and job title across the top of a sheet of paper. Under it, list all the ways the investment will specifically help his department. Maybe the system is far better at tracking demographic data. Maybe it will give him more up-to-the-moment information on the effect of regional promotions. It might give him greater access to his marketing staff across the country.

Now these may not be the advantages of the new system that happen to get you excited. As far as you're concerned, these advantages to marketing may even seem like minor plusses. But in framing, *your* perspective is not the important one. It's your listener's perspective that counts. As you prepare to describe the project and its outcomes to the marketing vice president, frame as much of the investment's outcomes around advantages geared specifically to marketing.

Or, if the person at the top of that list is from finance, ask yourself:

1. How specifically might my proposal be helpful to finance? Is it neutral or disadvantageous? Are there creative solutions to any disadvantages that would be appealing to finance?
2. What investments (e.g., time, resources, etc.) must he make? Will these be seen as reasonable to him? Will he perceive the overall return to be well worth the investment? How will he perceive the level of risk—the likelihood of the initiative's success or failure?
3. How can I realistically position my solution and outcomes as a gain for him? If this is difficult to achieve given the current plan, how might I change or adapt my approach/solution? What areas am I willing to compromise on? What areas do I feel I must hold firm on, and what is the level of risk if I do?

Exercise Two

You may want to be even more thorough in your preparation. Here's an exercise that will take you deeper into the mindset of your colleagues.

1. Set up two chairs facing one another in your office (or at home, if you don't have privacy at the office). Sit in one of

them. Make believe the person you're sizing up is sitting in the other.

2. Now talk to this person, telling him the positive outcomes that will result from your initiative. As you talk, note these outcomes on a sheet of paper.

3. Then switch to the other seat. Make believe you're that person. Have him speak to you from his perspective.

   Have him describe the key advantages and disadvantages he sees for himself in your proposal. For him, what are the potential rewards?

   Does the proposal speak to any shared values or beliefs?

   What is the language or terminology he naturally uses?

Note the answers to these questions on the sheet of paper.

When this imaginary conversation is over, compare the two lists. What you are looking for are areas of overlap on the positive side. Is there a central theme shared by both you and the other person? If yes, this common ground will become the general frame around which to build your position.

In the exercise, you might discover that both of you are concerned about growing a certain market, or reducing costs, or ensuring a faster response on customer service. It is around these theme areas that you must build your arguments and evidence.

Don't build them from what you see as positive outcomes for yourself if these are not shared by your colleague.

When it comes time to persuade him, make sure to incorporate any of the special values, beliefs, or terminology you noted.

Case in Point:
How Nina Found Common Ground

Nina felt strongly that the office needed a new accounting software system. The existing one was already eight years old and antiquated. She had four key individuals to persuade: Raj, Scott, Rachel, and Ping. Using the two-chairs exercise, she began to explore how each individual would respond to her proposal.

She started with Raj, the office accountant. She knew he would be full of glowing positives about the proposal. After all, it directly benefited him. As she played Raj, she learned that just about any positive argument would work with him, but that he would naturally expect to be heavily involved in deciding on the software package itself. Nina realized that to persuade him she had to involve Raj early on as a partner in the purchase.

Scott was the finance officer and was always reluctant to spend on anything. As she imagined what he would say, Nina began to realize that she couldn't persuade him on the features that she herself saw as the important improvements over the old system—easier entry of data, faster tabulations, special analysis, and presentation packages. These were what had sold Nina on the investment, but they wouldn't impress Scott. He needed to be convinced by the new system's ability to save the company substantial money beyond the cost of the investment itself. She would have to frame the issue around saving money. Nina made a note to get one of her best assistants to prepare a pro forma analysis of the software's potential cost savings. She knew this would take a few weeks to do well, but the wait was worth it if she could sell Scott.

Rachel was the office manager. Her main concerns were better tracking of accounts receivable, fewer system bugs in general, and speedier processing of financial statements to headquarters. Nina made another note. She'd have to ask the software consultants to provide a detailed report contrasting the company's old system with a new one along each of these dimensions. That's what would be decisive for Rachel.

Ping was the sales manager. He had often complained about how time consuming order entry was under the old system. He was cross that monthly sales reports were always late. These were the two areas around which Nina would have to frame her discussions with Ping to ensure that he would see the new system as a significant improvement over the old one.

She now had her general frames for each member of the team. For Raj, the system would have all the bells and whistles that he wanted. For Scott, the system would offer a substantial cost savings by reducing time consuming and often expensive administrative tasks required under the old system. For Rachel, a better tracking system with speedy report processing. For Ping, an easier system for data entry and on-time reports.

Nina set to work with her assistant and the computer consultant to find evidence to address each of these frames. These insights, Nina realized, were also helping her in designing a better system for everyone. Here was a surprising byproduct of learning how to be more persuasive. It was actually improving the quality of her solutions.

Table 2[10]
Summary of Basic American Values

1. The value of the individual
2. Achievement and success
3. Change and progress
4. Ethical equality
5. Equality of opportunity
6. Effort and optimism
7. Efficiency, practicality, and pragmatism
8. Rejection of authority
9. Science and secular rationality
10. Sociality
11. Material comfort
12. Quantification
13. External conformity
14. Humor
15. Generosity and "considerateness"
16. Patriotism

5
Compelling Positions and Evidence

What's the difference between a frame and the positions and evidence that support it?

Let's return to an example from the previous chapter. You will remember that Monica framed the issue of a new meal-pricing scheme around its ability to deliver greater profitability to the franchisees. The frame was: New meal scheme will lead to greater franchisee profitability.

To make this frame convincing, she used *evidence*—reports from a test market of the "whole meal" pricing scheme in Tennessee and from markets using medium-size meal packages throughout the U.S. outlets. This evidence showed that soft drink and fry sales actually increased in places where the new value meal was implemented. She also employed a second piece of evidence already widely known to her audience: These two product categories, fries and drinks, were among the most profitable. She then took these two pieces of evidence and *positioned* them together using a straightforward logic: If drink and fry sales increase under a value meal scheme, and if these are among our most profitable categories, then my frame is correct: The new scheme overall will lead to higher profitability for franchisees.

In essence, evidence is the facts and information we use to build compelling arguments for our frame. Positioning is how we structure, or logically organize, our evidence so that it leads our colleagues to the same conclusion we hold.

Here are typical questions we should ask ourselves about positions and evidence. They deal with the content and logic of our presentation:

1. What evidence do we have that clearly supports and builds our positions?
2. How can we order our evidence and arguments to be the most compelling?
3. Should we be addressing counterarguments?
4. Is there a simplicity to our logic that enhances comprehension?

Outside of the courtroom, most people tend to be somewhat ineffective in arranging and delivering their supporting positions and evidence. Yet research shows that the order, directness, and presence of counterarguments can have a powerful impact.

Another important aspect is the format and content of our positions and evidence. We should suit them to our audience. Some groups like to spend time in the details. Others prefer a compelling big picture. Some want objectivity, others want emotion. You have to size up your listeners.

Much of the time we are trying to persuade people that if they accept our proposition, a certain thing will happen in the future. A new pricing policy, for example, will increase profits. But the future has not yet occurred, of course, so our proposition is only as good as its evidence—its perceived accuracy and the probability of its occurring. Here lies the challenge—to select and craft evidence that makes our arguments about the future seem plausible and worthwhile.

At the same time, we want our colleagues truly to *identify* with our position. This depends upon our ability to present evidence and a position that draw colleagues into sharing our own convictions.

Positions and Evidence: Questions of Arrangement, Directness, and Counterarguments

When presenting our positions, we should put some thought into arranging our arguments for maximum effect. Fortunately, we're not flying blind. Over several decades there's been a good deal of research on the subject. I draw on that research when I deal with the questions I'm often asked about effective presentation. For example:

Should I Put My Strongest Evidence First or Last?

Extensive research shows it usually doesn't much matter when you deliver your most substantial firepower. But if you find yourself in a situation where you have little time to talk and where others can freely interrupt and discuss your points, then saving the best arguments for last may create a problem. Time may run out and you may never get a chance to present those arguments. In which case, your best arguments should come up front.[1]

Should I Make My Points Directly or Indirectly?

Sometimes we wonder whether we should make our points very clearly or more subtly, making them implicit rather than explicit.

In the latter case, we are hoping that our audience will draw the conclusions we want them to by themselves: We'd supply them with a few key hints or indirect points, and they'd see the light. They'd be more deeply convinced because they'd have seemed to reach the conclusions on their own.

On the other hand, if we present clear conclusions, we're less likely to leave our audience in confusion or in doubt as to what we believe.

This issue has been the subject of innumerable investigations. The vast majority of studies show that explicit conclusions or recommendations are more persuasive than ones that are only hinted at. It's important in our persuasion, therefore, to make our conclusions clear.[2] This is not to say that these clear statements should be made up front, at the outset of our attempts to persuade. As we've seen earlier, they're sometimes best reserved for a while. Otherwise we risk provoking opposition early on.

Should I Address Counterpositions or Ignore Them?

You know that some of your colleagues will object to some of the things you want to say. You wonder if you should speak to those objections before they're even made.

You could try to knock them down preemptively by stating your views very strongly, avoiding any statement that might give them ammunition. Or you might try a two-sided approach, raising the objections that might possibly be made and dealing with them one by one.

As it turns out, two-sided persuasion is generally the best approach. Addressing opposing viewpoints directly is often the more effective and convincing approach for an educated audience of people who are probably aware of the counterarguments. It demonstrates a realism that makes our viewpoint seem all the more credible. It overcomes any perceptions that we are naïve or blind to other perspectives.

Experiments have also been conducted to see if the ways in which two-sided messages are organized can influence an audience. For example, there are three possible ways to present a two-sided message: *(1)* our supporting arguments first and then arguments refuting the counterarguments; *(2)* refuting counterarguments first, then our supporting arguments; or *(3)* interweaving the two. What the evidence shows is that option number one (the supporting, then refuting approach) and also number three (the interspersing technique) are generally the more effective.[3]

Building in Hidden Attractions
for Persuasive Appeal

The father of the science of persuasion, Aristotle, pointed out that the most persuasive positions were the ones that most actively involved the listener, the ones in which the listener—drawing upon what he already knows and believes—actually becomes part of the process of building the position.

This kind of extra-strength persuasion happens when there's shared ground between the persuader and the listener. Perhaps it's a belief (high-performance targets are motivating), a goal (striving to have a balanced life), or a value (we should treat staff members equally). Since this is shared ground, it does not need to be expressed. Instead the listeners fill it in by themselves if the position is carefully constructed by the person doing the persuading.[4]

When there's shared ground, the skillful persuader can connect it to the conclusion he wants his listeners to reach. The persuader knows that if he mentions beliefs his audience shares—say, that high-performance goals motivate and his listeners know that many employees have low to mid-range goals—he can be sure his listeners, "on their own," will reach the conclusion he wants them to: that many employees are not highly motivated.

Once again let's take Monica's proposition to her franchisees. The logic of her arguments can be arranged as follows:

1. Whole-meal pricing in a Tennessee test site and medium-size meal packages in U.S. outlets increased drink and fry sales.
2. Drinks and fries sales are the franchisees' highest profit categories.
3. Therefore whole-meal pricing in Canadian outlets will mean greater franchise profitability.

So what is the unexpressed shared ground that links these arguments in her audience's mind? It's that the Canadian marketplace is similar to that of the United States. Whatever happens in the U.S. will be mirrored in Canada. In reality, this may not be an accurate assumption, but it is the assumption held by Monica's audience. So the audience ends up drawing Monica's last conclusion (number three, above) by using this element of their own reasoning. Because they felt they drew the conclusion on their own, they were convinced all the more powerfully. Our challenge then is to find the unspoken beliefs, goals, and values of our colleagues that will lead them to our conclusions.

Presentation and Content: Tailoring Positions and Evidence to Our Audience

Many of us have preferences when it comes to the way we receive information. Some like memos; some want to be faxed or e-mailed; some want to hear you say it. It's the same when people are being persuaded; they differ in the kinds of approaches that work with them. It's wise to know these preferences before we start to persuade. If we do, we can tailor our positions and evidence in the ways that resonate with each colleague.

Katherine Briggs and her daughter, Isabel Myers, were keen observers of human personality. Drawing on the ideas of noted Swiss psychologist Carl Jung, they developed and refined over a span of fifty years a system for classifying people by their decision-making styles. Called the Myers-Briggs Type, it has two dimensions that are useful in thinking about persuasion approaches.[5]

Dimension number one divides people into two groups: We incline toward being either *sensing* people, says Myers-Briggs, or *intuitive* people.[6]

Sensors are people who are very concerned about the details of a project. They require lots of "hard" facts to be convinced. The more we can go into the fine points and specifics, the happier they are. The more concrete the specifics, the better. They are natural pragmatists and will focus on the "here and now" realities in what the persuader is presenting.

Intuitives, however, want the big picture. They're interested in the ideas behind the project and in its future benefits. They are somewhat less pragmatic, less concerned with the details. The things that impress them in a presentation are new possibilities, inspiration, and imagination.

Myers-Briggs dimension number two splits people between *thinkers* and *feelers.*[7]

Thinking people like to see a strongly rational approach in any presentation we make to them. They want us to move logically from point to point and to list the costs and benefits of our proposal objectively. They'll look carefully at the links we make, in our evidence, between cause and effect. What sells them will be not so much our feelings as our objective thinking.

Feeling people want to know what our plan's impact will be on others. They care a great deal about the effect it will have on the human side of the organization. In our presentations, they often respond to the values and principles behind our positions.

Our challenge is to figure out what types we're talking to and shape our presentations accordingly. At the end of the chapter you'll find Exhibits 7 and 8, which illustrate the essential differences. There is also a list of questions you can use to distinguish sensing people from the intuitives and feeling people from the thinking types.

Most of us lean in one direction or the other along these two dimensions. For example, I am an intuitive thinker. Someone else might be a sensing thinker or an intuitive feeler.

It is important to remember that you and I are strongly influenced by our own Myers-Briggs orientation. Whatever it is it will lead us to assemble certain types of evidence and describe our position in a certain way. For example, as an intuitive type, I might present ideas and their ramifications as the appealing features of my position. I may not spend a great deal of time building my case with lots of details.

My orientation, however, may not be the orientation of the colleague I am trying to persuade. She may be a sensing type, who'd impatiently await nitty-gritty details while I went on and on about the big picture. Meanwhile, my fellow intuitives in the audience would feel quite comfortable with my approach; to them it might feel quite attractive and natural.

Decide what type you are and consider how that orientation may be shaping your persuasion without your being aware of it.

Decide what types your colleagues are and make sure you give them the kind of material they're programmed to desire.

Finding a Simple Logic to Convey Our Positions and Evidence

You are sitting down to prepare for today's meeting. You have outlined lots of ideas. You want to make sure everyone understands them and sees the logic behind them. You want to be thoroughly convincing. You think to yourself: "If I want to persuade these people, I'd better give them all the ammunition I can, all the facts and statistics."

Sorry. You're already on the wrong track. You're on your way to robbing your ideas of power and losing your audience at the same time. The old saying "Include much, impress little" sums up what you're about to do. Remember that people's brains are already chockablock full of information. Your challenge is to obtain "mind share" in a crowded market.

In order to do this, each of us has to break one bad habit. That habit is throwing as much information as possible at our audience. What do you suppose happens when you force-feed the minds of human beings with lots of information? Unless they are unusually motivated to listen, their minds go inert—in other words, they get bored or lose track of what we're saying. They start thinking about other things. So most effective persuaders choose just a few very convincing arguments and rely on those. They distill their message into several central, often simple, themes and thread them throughout their presentation. Evidence is powerful but not excessive.

Why is simplicity so important? Much of it has to do with the physiology of the brain. While blessed with this remarkable organ, human beings in reality have a limited capacity to store and recall information. Our brains simply cannot hold in "active memory" every bit of information they receive in a given moment. Herbert Simon, a Nobel laureate and social scientist from Carnegie-Mellon University, described the situation: "The world is constantly drenching us with information through eyes and ears—millions of bits per second."[8]

This flood should overwhelm us. But the brain in its brilliance has evolved ways to select the information it considers useful and discard the rest. When someone is talking to us, the mind is automatically attempting to shrink down the incoming information to as few points as possible. For example, there you are in a meeting, listening to the boss present a marketing plan. While your brain is processing what he is saying, it is also wondering whether you should lend your son the car this evening, worrying about a problem employee, and calculating the calories from a slice of cheesecake you had at lunch. All of this is going on simultaneously.

How can anyone remember all the points made at a meeting? They can't. George Miller, at Harvard, and his colleagues discovered that on average individuals could hold in short-term memory, *without forgetting*, only six or seven pieces of data. Members of a typical audience will remember as little as 10 percent of a presentation, and the most effective speakers can increase retention to only as high as 50 percent. Even if you're the best, half of what you say is gone.[9]

The challenge, of course, is getting people to remember your key points instead of something else.

There is another force at play, which demands that we powerfully simplify what we are presenting. Our attention spans are shrinking, and dramatically so. Only a century ago a typical political speech could run up to two hours without losing its audience. Today's audiences can put up with only a small fraction of that amount. Movies now are constructed so that only a few minutes will pass before there is a change of scene to snag our fleeting attention. Commercials are about fifteen seconds. Television and our hectic pace—both have encouraged a restlessness in industrialized countries that is profoundly altering our willingness to stay focused for any length of time.

The same phenomenon is affecting communications in management. The other day, the training director of one company lamented to me that today's managers could sit still for a maximum of half an hour of class time before growing restless. Fifteen years ago, he explained, that same class could have gone on for an hour and a half without restlessness. We can begin to understand why "sound bytes" are so popular—those ten-second messages designed to capture your attention with an unforgettable phrase. All this means is that you and I have to work hard to get people's attention. So how do we do it?

The first thing to know is that the brain is a little lazy. While it welcomes challenges and puzzles, as we will see, it is drawn toward a delivery that is focused. It likes simplicity. You can take advantage of that brain attribute by presenting your ideas with greater clarity. I've found that the best way to do this is to ask ourselves:

- What is the core idea I wish to communicate today?
- If I were forced to summarize everything I wanted to say in two or three statements, what would they be?
- What would be the few principal arguments and most compelling evidence I'd pick to support them?

The finest example of tactical simplicity I've come across in my career as a management professor and consultant is *Let's Get in There and Fight!*, known as The Little Red Book, produced by SAS airlines and its president, Jan Carlzon. In the early 1980s, Carlzon was made CEO of the airline operations of Scandinavian Airlines System.[10] After seventeen profitable years, SAS was then suffering its second year of losses. Instead of a strategy of cost cutting, Carlzon decided on a new-growth approach. He gave SAS the mission of becoming "the best airline in the world for the frequent business traveler." As Carlzon explained:

> The result was a unique strategy plan for turning the company around. Far from cutting costs more, we proposed to the SAS board that we invest an additional $45 million and increase operating expenses by $12 million a year for 147 different projects including launching a comprehensive punctuality campaign, improving our traffic hub in Copenhagen, offering service courses for more than 12,000 of our staff, and restoring the olive in our customers' martinis. It was an enormous risk. The greater challenge was to persuade SAS employees that this new strategy was the right one. Historically, service had taken a back seat in the company. Now suddenly,

under the new strategy, everyone in the company was to be focused foremost on customer service.

Carlzon wanted a vehicle to convey the company's new vision very simply yet make it seem vitally necessary. He needed a compelling logic, one that could be understood by the company's twenty thousand employees and persuasive at the same time. So he wrote a little book, titled it *Let's Get in There and Fight!*, had it bound in red, and distributed it to everyone in SAS. Carlzon explained his reasoning: "We wanted everyone to understand the goal; we couldn't risk our message becoming distorted as it worked its way through the company."

You'll find pages from *Let's Get in There and Fight!* reproduced at the end of this book (Appendix 3). They show how Carlzon approached the task he set out for himself.

His remarkably short opening letter lays out quite clearly the dilemmas facing SAS (Exhibit 1). Through a minimum of words and some simple cartoonlike pictures he then lays out all the threats to the airline (Exhibit 2). He discusses the competition from American carriers like Delta and European carriers like Swissair (Exhibit 3). Then, with a graph, he introduces a few key statistics —benchmarking SAS against the above two primary competitors (Exhibit 4). From this one graph, employees can see how severe the situation is, but no one at SAS is blamed.

He portrays the situation in such simple terms that even a janitor at SAS can comprehend the company's plight. Statistics are kept to a minimum, again to ensure maximum reach and comprehension.

Running throughout is a thread of optimism: "I am convinced . . . we have the know-how." There is also a thread of urgency: "We are going to lose money this year, too. But then, it's got to stop. We can't afford to lose any more!"

We have to beat them, he says, and we'll do it through customer service. Then he lists the steps essential to survival, the behavior and attitude changes it will take to succeed (Exhibit 5). To make his ambitious plan seem feasible, not daunting, he states that in the first year only a 2 percent improvement is required (Exhibit 6).

What Carlzon does is to take what in reality is an enormous challenge and make it seem doable.

Now contrast this approach with what most companies would do. In attempting to persuade their organizations about a new corporate strategy, most would produce a thick document detailing in great complexity and with innumerable statistics why a new strategy is called for. The follow-up presentations to the organization at large would mirror the original in their complexity. As a result, general comprehension of the new strategy would be low and support for it, below the executive level, paltry.

Carlzon, instead, in his unconventional style, created arguments and plans that even the SAS maintenance crew standing on the airport tarmac could understand and be persuaded by. And that is exactly what happened. The whole company got behind the customer-service drive, and gradually SAS's market share improved. In the second year the airline returned to profitability.

Exhibit 1

We have to fight in a stagnating market.

We have to fight competitors who are more efficient than we are.

And who are at least as good as we are in figuring out the best deals.

We can do it. But only if we are prepared to fight. Side by side.

We are all in this together.

Jan Carlzon

Exhibit 2

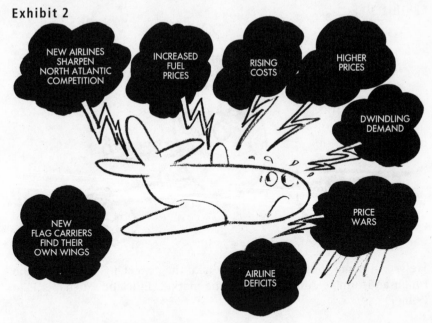

Suddenly, bad weather struck . . .

The airline lost $12 million last year.
We are going to lose money this year, too.
But then it's got to stop. We can't afford to lose any more!

Exhibit 3

We've got some tough competition. Like the "street fighters" from the rough-and-tumble American domestic market. Efficient. In shape. Like Delta . . .

Or European companies which have pursued more consistent and purposeful policies than we have. And who keep making money, hard times or not.

Exhibit 4

Look at the differences:

Key figures *	Swissair INTERNATIONAL	SAS INTERNATIONAL
Cabin Factor	63.6	59.3
Load Factor	59.2	57.8
Passenger revenue (USD)/RPK	0.09	0.08
Cargo revenue (USD)/RFTK	0.37	0.31
Total revenue (USD)RTK	0.79	0.73
Operating cost (USD)/ATK	0.45	0.42
Revenue-Cost Relationship (Over 100—pront)	103.5	99.7
Average flight leg/km	1051	967

* USD—U.S. Dollars. RPK—Revenue Passenger-kilometers, RFTK—Revenue Freight Tonne-kilometers. RTK—Revenue Tonne-kilometers. ATK—Available Tonne-kilometers.
Exchange rate: one USD—4.65 Swedish kronor.

Delta has:

○ 40% more revenue tonne-kms per employee

○ 120% more passengers per employee

○ 14% more available tonne-kms per pilot

○ 40% more passenger-kms per cabin attendant

○ 35% more passenger-kms per passenger sales employee

It is difficult to make similar comparisons in the technical and maintenance fields, but even in these areas Delta has a substantially higher productivity than SAS.

Exhibit 5

This is how we are going to do it!

We have to be more efficient.

We have to consolidate.   We have to be market-oriented.

We are going to consolidate!

○ With fewer aircraft types

○ With a "cleaner" network

○ With more profitable routes

This will help cut our costs.

Exhibit 5 (Contd.)

This is what we're going to do for Business Class:

Ticket Offices
Special phone numbers.
High-level service at ticket counters.

Check-in
Simplified check-in for passengers
with carry-on baggage only.
Separate check-in counters for
Business Class.
Seat selection.
High service level, shorter lines.
Quicker check-in procedures.
Special baggage tags.

Service Lounge at Kastrup
Telephone, telex services (debited).
Ticketing (Help with rebookings).
Office space.
Coffee shop.
SAS News Bulletin Board.
Wardrobe for winter clothes.
Message Service.

Embarkation
Economy Class passengers board first.
Business class passengers board last.
Gate manager to assist passengers.

Debarkation
Business Class first.

We are going to be much more punctual. Everyone can help.

"Operation Punctuality" is starting soon. It's going to give everyone a chance to help make us one of Europe's most punctual airlines.

Exhibit 6

When you put it all together . . .   . . . that should do it.

- ○ We are slashing unnecessary costs.

- ○ We are improving our efficiency.

- ○ We are consolidating our operations and cutting even more costs.

- ○ We are tailoring our products and service for the needs of the big business travel market, to increase our income.

- ○ We are boosting our profitability with cargo and tourism.

- ○ We are grabbing every opportunity for marginal business.

- ○ We are going to find it's more fun to work.

+2%

A 2% improvement means some $30 million. With that much in our pockets, we've taken the first step toward a new, profitable SAS.

Heightening the Plausibility and Attractiveness of Our Positions and Evidence

In persuasion, we want our colleagues to feel that our position and evidence are not only plausible but compelling. There are several devices that can help us make them feel that way. They all illustrate our points but in differing ways.

Examples

The use of examples is one of the oldest tools of persuasion and a highly effective way to present evidence.

If the examples are good, your listeners will generalize from them to the outcome you're predicting. Talking to executives about managing change, I will often use case examples from the experience of other companies. The executives relate those examples to their own companies. They begin to think that if the change worked for those other firms, it might work for theirs.

The power of an example lies in its reality; it's a slice of real life, specific rather than abstract. It helps our colleagues deal with the uncertain (the outcome we are predicting) by connecting it to something concrete and familiar (the example).

In one study it was discovered that of all the possible types of arguments, those based on examples are the least vulnerable to being refuted. Other research showed that when arguments are based on case histories, listeners remember them better and are more likely to be influenced by them.[11]

As I just noted, examples are particularly useful when we are trying to assure listeners of how something will work out in the future—the majority of persuasion situations. They can powerfully affect our listeners' expectations. A marketing manager, trying to persuade senior executives to invest in a new product, might cite examples of similar past investments in new products that paid off handsomely. In reality, the marketing manager cannot be absolutely certain of this outcome. In addition, the parallel example may have occurred under very different circumstances. But by tying his position to past examples that are perceived to be similar, he can heighten the perception that the same outcomes are likely to reoccur.

To understand why examples work so well in framing, we can turn to the work of psychologist George A. Kelly. He argued that as human beings we continually attempt to predict events. We do so according to our past experience. If we feel we can't predict, we feel we lack control and are helpless. To gain a sense of control, we take the seemingly random occurrences of life and try to make sense out of them, to see some sort of meaning. We focus on general features of these events and hope that from these we can identify patterns. The events are our examples, and the patterns we see in events are our generalizations, by which we try to predict repetitions of similar events in the future.[12]

Karen Fries of Microsoft (chapter 3) drew upon innumerable case examples of software users to illustrate the desperate need for more user-friendly computer interfaces. In one memo, she described how a Microsoft employee who was trying to create a publication struggled with a zoom control. The problem was that the zooming function was hidden on the menu. Her most effective example, however, was the case of the man who grabbed Karen by the arm during a product demonstration of BOB. His exclamation—that Microsoft could save all of the money it spends on manuals but just give him the little animated character to help him—had dramatic appeal. Real-life examples such as these were extremely useful in Karen's persuasion.

Since examples make the listener our partner in constructing our positions, it's important that we choose ones that reflect common experiences and are likely to prompt the same shared interpretations. It is also important that we not present too many examples because this tends to overload the listener's attention and makes our position appear formal and technical.[13]

Analogies

You remember that back in chapter 2, when I talked about the automobile vice president who wanted to shift to a V-6, I suddenly began talking about the circus. I told how lion tamers use a chair to deal with lions.

At that point in the exercise you may have been wondering what lions had to do with automobiles and how I'd ever tie this circus thing into the larger subject under discussion. But I did it, I think. I said an executive making a difficult presentation could learn something from a lion tamer: Both are well advised to give their adversaries as little as possible to grab on to.

That was my notorious lion tamer analogy. Analogies capitalize on a relationship of likeness between two things—often very unlike things, such as executives and lion tamers. They're used to make a point vivid, to clarify it, or to stimulate certain emotions. They are a terrific tool in persuasion. They let us convey the logic of our arguments very simply and powerfully, using experiences familiar to our listeners. They tend to bypass the mind and appeal to the emotions.

Jack Welch, CEO of General Electric, wanted to persuade his employees to embrace simplicity in their decision making and turn away from complexity. He used these two analogies:

- Simplicity is a quality sneered at today in cultures that like their business concepts the way they like their wine . . . full of nuance . . . subtlety . . . complexity . . . with hints of this and that.
- In the '90s, cultures like that will produce sophisticated decisions loaded with nuance and complexity that arrive at the station long after the train has gone.[14]

Wine tasting and missing the train is a particularly rich analogy because the wine-taster image conveys the notion of pretense, of decision makers who like complexity for its own sake and assume they are sophisticated yet in reality are fallible. Welch is telling his organization to turn its back on such behavior or else the competition will quickly overtake General Electric. GE will miss the train.

Analogies are especially powerful in communicating ideas and goals—more powerful, often, than arguments supported by logic and statistics. Yet corporations and MBA programs encourage the latter—carefully planned managerial presentations supported by mountains of statistical information. While such presentations are critical to effective decision making, this uptight, fact-ridden style has become so ingrained that managers tend to use it exclusively, even in speeches, pep talks, and discussions with customers and analysts. Maybe even with their spouses and kids. I know many effective leaders, however, who refuse to forfeit the punch they can give their communications, in any situation, with a good analogy, image, or story. If it's a tool that works—and it does—they pick it up and use it.

Why does it work so well? Research in speech communications shows that analogies excite the imagination of the listener. First they create a state of tension (puzzlement, perhaps, or recoil), then tension release (insight and resolution). The listener isn't just a passive receiver of information; he's triggered into a state of active thinking as he puzzles over the meaning of the story and attempts to make sense of it. This process is so engaging that it makes for listener attention and interest. (For a persuader, winning attention and interest is what it's all about.)[15]

Other studies explain why these rhetorical devices are a more effective way to convey ideas. They've found that people treat statistical summaries as if they were largely *uninformative*. Statistics lack impact because they're abstract, colorless. The studies indicate that information is absorbed by listeners in proportion to its vividness.[16] Also, that the vividness of analogies produces much more memory recall than literal descriptions do.

Karen Fries should win a medal for the wonderful analogy she used when persuading Microsoft of the need for BOB and its super-simple help approach. Here's what she said:

> Imagine you want to cook a dinner and that you must first go to the supermarket. There's all the flexibility you want—you can cook anything in the world as long as you know how, and you have the time and desire to do it.
>
> First you need to know what you want to do. You find all these overstuffed aisles with cryptic single-word headings like "sundries" and "ethnic food" and "condiments." These are [analogous to] the menus on our [pres-

ent] computer interfaces. The question, of course, is whether salt is under condiments or ethnic food or behind the potato chip section. There are surrounding racks and wall spaces, much as our software interfaces now have support buttons, tool bars, and lines around the perimeters.

Now after you have hunted and collected everything, you still need to put it all together in the correct order to make a meal. If you are a good cook, you will probably get a good meal. If you're a novice, [you will] probably not [get a good meal]. We [at Microsoft] have been selling under the supermarket category for years, and we [Karen's team] think there is a big opportunity for restaurants.

If you want a good meal in a relaxing ambiance, restaurants are the ticket. That's what we are trying to do now with BOB: pushing the next step with software that is more like going to a restaurant . . . so the user does not spend all their time searching for the ingredients.

We [the software] are instead the active ones. We find and put the ingredients together. You sit down, you get comfortable. We bring you a menu. The meal is organized around categories, like pasta or chicken! It's easy to find what you want if you wish to create a newsletter. You simply tell us you want so-and-so type of newsletter. You don't have to come [to the table] with any information, you can choose what you want. How the dish is exactly created is not important. We do the work, you relax. It's an enjoyable experience. No walking around lost trying to find things, no cooking.

As you read through Karen's brilliant analogy, you can feel how much more powerfully this parallel idea of a supermarket conveys our problems with conventional software. Its power comes directly from our personal experiences. We all know the frustration of searching up and down grocery aisles, so when Karen links it to the frustration of searching for functions on our computers, the latter becomes vivid to us. We also know the ease and pleasure of restaurant dining. It's an experience we enjoy, and we unconsciously transfer these positive feelings to Karen's proposal about BOB. The analogy compels us to support her.

Now imagine if Karen had attempted to convey her position through a literal description of BOB's advantages. Since few in her audience of highly computer-literate Microsoft employees would have had the menu-searching frustration that BOB was designed to eliminate, the problem wouldn't have been vivid to them, and they wouldn't have appreciated the market for BOB. Also, without the supermarket and restaurant analogy, Karen's presentation would have felt far more technical and mechanical. There would be none of the accompanying emotions of frustration and pleasure, which do much of the persuading for her.

Karen's pictures of supermarkets and restaurants conjure up rich feelings and reactions for us. This is a masterful use of analogy to persuade.

Stories

You may have noted that I've used stories extensively throughout this book to illustrate ideas and capture your attention. They are like examples except they have a plot and may not always describe actual events. Stories are the oldest forms of conveying information and can be particularly compelling. They are a powerful means of getting listeners to identify with our position, because a well-crafted story will at some level involve colleagues emotionally, the way analogies do. Stories also possess the vividness quality we discussed earlier. Finally, they deliver our message in a more casual manner; they invite our listeners to pay attention but not to feel pushed or commanded.

One of the great masters of storytelling for persuasion is the noted trial lawyer Gerry Spence. He has never lost a criminal trial in his career, and his cases have included such notables as Karen Silkwood and Imelda Marcos. If we look carefully at how he persuades, we find he does it in large part with stories. "Every argument," he says, "in court or out, whether delivered over the supper table or made at coffee break, can be reduced to a story. An argument, like a house, yes, like the houses of the three little pigs, has structure. Whether it will fall, whether it can be blown down when the wolf huffs and puffs, depends upon how the house has been built. The strongest structure for any argument is [a] *story.*"[17]

In his book *How to Argue and Win Every Time,* Spence gives many examples of how he poses his positions in story form. "Suppose you want to petition the county commissioners to construct a new road to replace an existing dangerous one," he says.

> You could argue that the county commissioners have the duty to provide safe ingress and egress for the taxpayers, and that the present road is inherently unsafe and does not conform to minimum highway standards. You could quote the standards and cite the specifics of how the road is in violation of those standards. Or, you could provide the commissioners with the following argument that takes the form of a story:
>
> "I was driving down Beach Creek Road today. I had my four-year-old daughter Sarah with me. I strapped her as tightly into the seat as I could, because I knew the road could be very dangerous, and I strapped myself in as well. Although this was a dangerous road, it was the only one Sarah and I could take to town.
>
> "As usual, I drove very slowly, hugging the shoulder all the way. As I was coming to that first blind curve, I thought, *What would happen to us if a drunk comes around that corner on the wrong side of the road? What would happen to us if a speeding driver came barreling around that curve and slid slightly over the center line? There would be no escape for us.* The shoulder is narrow. There is a deep drop-off. I looked at my little daughter and I thought, *This isn't fair to her. She is innocent. Why should she be subjected to this danger?*
>
> "And then when I was well into the curve I saw the approaching vehicle. A lot of thoughts flashed through my mind. I recalled there had been four deaths on this road in the past ten years, and I don't know how many wrecks that resulted in serious injury. I thought, *Based on*

the number of deaths per thousand persons in this war zone, a
person would have had a much better chance to survive in
Vietnam.

"As you can see, this time Sarah and I made it. This
time the driver wasn't drunk. This time the driver was
attentive. This time the driver was in control of his car,
but there wasn't much room to spare when we met. I
could have reached out and touched the side of his car.
The question is, When will Sarah and I become just another statistic on this road? Will you remember us? Will
you remember me standing here imploring you to do
something about this? Especially for her? Please?" [18]

The argument creates word images of innocent people—especially a child—trapped in inescapable danger. It touches the emotions of the commissioners, who have the power and therefore the
responsibility. "Will you remember me standing here imploring
you to do something about this?" are powerful word weapons that
will not be forgotten.

The story adds a dramatic vividness to the message. By creative exaggeration, he conveys his central idea: The road should be
improved. The story is designed to grab the commissioners' attention. As he says, he could have lectured them on their duties under
the law. Instead, he let a gripping story do his persuading for him.

Another master of stories for persuasion purposes is management guru Tom Peters. When Peters is selling his audiences on
new management ideas, he creates a string of stories to support his
basic points. He believes that the stories that work most effectively
with business people must be mixed with data, and that ultimately
we are convinced by numbers, but numbers presented in story
form.

Details, he stresses, are important. He fills his stories with
specifics such as names and addresses and sense impressions. What
did it look like? What did it sound like? [19]

Stories can be particularly potent when they invoke meanings
or symbols that have deep cultural roots. Turning to one of the
most dramatic speeches of all time, Steven Jobs' presentation to
the Boston Computer Society introducing the Macintosh com-

puter, we see how Jobs' use of cultural stories positioned Apple as the David and IBM as the Goliath of the computer world a decade ago. Jobs began his talk dramatically in an Orwellian voice:

It is 1958. IBM passes up the chance to buy a young, fledgling company that has just invented a new technology, called xerography. Two years later Xerox is born, and IBM has been kicking themselves ever since.

It is ten years later. The late '60s. Digital Equipment Corporation and others invent the mini-computer. IBM dismisses the mini-computer as too small to do serious computing, and therefore unimportant to their business. DEC grows to become a multi-hundred-million-dollar corporation before IBM finally enters the mini-computer market.

It is now ten years later. The late '70s. In 1977, Apple, a young, fledgling company on the West Coast invents the Apple II, the first personal computer as we know it today. IBM dismisses the personal computer as too small to do serious computing and therefore unimportant to their business.

The early 1980s. 1981. Apple II has become the world's most popular computer, and Apple has grown to a 300 million dollar corporation, becoming the fastest growing company in American business history. With over 50 companies vying for a share, IBM enters the personal computer market in November of 1981, with the IBM PC. In 1983, Apple and IBM emerge as the industry's strongest competitors, each selling approximately one billion dollars worth of personal computers in 1983. Each will invest greater than 50 million dollars for R & D and another 50 million for television advertising in 1984, totaling almost one quarter of a billion dollars combined.

The shake-out is in full swing. The first major firm goes bankrupt with others teetering on the brink. Total industry losses for 1983 overshadow even the combined profits of Apple and IBM for personal computers.

It is now 1984. It appears IBM wants it all. Apple is perceived to be the only hope to offer IBM a run for its money. Dealers, initially welcoming IBM with open arms, now fear an IBM-dominated and -controlled future. They're increasingly turning back to Apple as the only force that can ensure their future freedom. IBM wants it all, and is aiming its guns on its last obstacle to industry control—Apple. Will Big Blue dominate the entire computer industry? The entire information age? Was George Orwell right? [20]

In his speech, Jobs casts the Apple-IBM competition as a narrative, the story of the underdog forces of good (Apple), which must fight and triumph against the forces of evil (IBM). The listener, at some level, cues into emotional associations—feelings of positive regard for Apple, its difficult task, and its courage. Negative feelings are fostered toward the mammoth IBM that attempts to crush this positive force.

Other associations are triggered. The references to George Orwell's book *1984*, widely popular among the young of Jobs' generation, evoke the image of a Big Brother–like menacing giant (IBM) who is seeking omnipresent control. The word "freedom," for many, summons up historical associations with the American Revolution and the nation's fight against British domination, again feeding into the theme of the underdog Apple triumphing over tyrannical forces.

Through links to these important cultural stories, Jobs fills his audience with enthusiastic emotions toward Apple and strong negative feelings toward IBM.

How can each of us devise stories that fit what we are arguing? To answer that question, I asked another great storyteller, the motivational speaker Zig Ziglar, where he obtained the many stories in his speeches. He told me that he read newspapers extensively looking for relevant events or new research to illustrate his points. He also explained that everyday events were a particularly rich source and that he gleaned many of these during walks.

"I do my most creative thinking when I'm walking," he said. "Let me give you a simple little example of seeing stories. The other morning I was out walking, and I went under a highway overpass. There's a major thoroughfare above, and a tunnel underneath it. Well, there were two little girls riding their bikes, and they were having a little difficulty pedaling their bikes up the incline in this tunnel. One of them turned and said, 'I don't like riding up hills.' At that moment, it occurred to me that in life very few of us really enjoy going up hills. But it's the only time we really learn and develop. That's when we find out who we are and what we're capable of doing. This is just a little example of how I like to watch events take place [that can then become stories]."

Zig would later use that story in his talks on how individuals learn and are motivated. Many of his other stories come from his own life.

One important rule for storytelling is to choose stories that our listeners will understand. Subjects they can't relate to aren't of much use.

Spence recommends that we write out our stories beforehand in some detail. This allows us to think through the story's nuances carefully and to tailor these nuances to our principal argument.

In the practice sessions at the end of this chapter, you'll find questions to ask yourself as you prepare to persuade. Your thoughtful, painstaking answers to them will boost the chances that your persuasion will succeed.

Practice Session: How to Develop Compelling Positions and Evidence

Exercise One: Tailoring Presentations to Your Colleagues

When attempting persuasion, the first step is always to understand the colleague you are about to persuade. In this case, I want you to pay careful attention to how your colleague presents his ideas and proposals when he himself is trying to persuade. It may offer valuable clues about what he considers persuasive.

If you can identify his Myers-Briggs Type (see page 131), you'll have a handle on how to deal with him. Does he use lots of details and tangible evidence? This would suggest the Myers-Briggs Type called Sensor.

Or is he inclined to talk about the big-picture advantages of his ideas and be quite conceptual in describing outcomes? If so, he is probably an Intuitive.

Is he highly rational in his presentations, following a thoughtful line of point-by-point logic? This would suggest a Thinker.

Or does he rely more on his emotions to sell his ideas, and on an appeal to values and principles? Then he's most likely a Feeler.

When you identify your colleague's Myers-Briggs Type, refer to Exhibits 1 and 2 for suggestions on how to approach that type. What you must do is mirror as best you can, when you present your ideas to him, the style he prefers. If he prefers details, focus on the details. If he's highly logical, use a clear point-by-point logic to convey your initiative.

Just as you must sometimes employ a different style for different colleagues, you must tailor your evidence to your listener. Evidence that one colleague would find convincing may not convince another. As you are reviewing the evidence you need to build a compelling picture for your position, walk yourself through the following questions:

1. For each colleague: What would be a few, highly convincing pieces of evidence that would incline him to support my position?

2. If I were to rank my evidence from strongest to weakest, what would that list look like? (You will want to follow this order when you actually start persuading: Begin with the strongest.)

3. What examples, analogies, and stories would further support and illustrate my evidence?

4. What important counterarguments could my colleagues be likely to make as I go along? (Prepare answers to each and then include these responses in your presentation beforehand. In this way, you proactively address concerns before they are raised in challenge to you.)

5. What type of positioning of my evidence would my colleagues find most compelling?

6. What would be a powerful conclusion that all would find convincing?

Finally, ask yourself:

1. Do I have plenty of time to discuss my points? If not, put your most compelling arguments up front.
2. Have I distilled my message into a straightforward and appealing logic in my colleague's eyes?
3. Are my recommendations clear and explicit?

Exercise Two: Finding the Right Examples

Examples can be a powerful part of effective persuasion. As you think about your persuasion situation, identify the categories of examples you will need in creating a highly convincing position. Then start your search. Using online services and scanning references for articles is one way. Another is simply to be on the lookout for usable stories and analogies as you go through your daily life. Always keep in mind the themes you're hoping to illustrate with a good story or image. While you're reading *The Wall Street Journal* or as you sit in meetings, you'll come across news items or hear anecdotes that make a point you want to make. If you're on the alert, you'll find items you can use.

Be sure to note these items down. You may think you won't forget them, but you might; and good evidence is too valuable to squander. Form the habit of carrying a small notebook, or of keeping 3 x 5 index cards in your shirt pocket. At the end of the day, transfer your notes to files you've created, with a topic heading for each initiative you'll be addressing.

Into these topical files also put supporting evidence in the form of articles, reports, and examples from the field that are pertinent to your initiative. It is important to be highly selective: Use only examples that clearly argue your case. Don't junk up your files with stuff that has only the vaguest relevance.

Next, think about your audience. Will the examples you have collected be understandable to everyone you'll be persuading? Or do you need to use different examples with different individuals? Are the examples sophisticated enough to be truly convincing for everyone? Screen out those that are not. The aim is to match carefully the examples we choose to the backgrounds and savvy of our colleagues.

See the case presented below, in which Jerry carefully chooses his evidence.

Exercise Three:
Analogies and Images that Convince

Finding the right analogy or image is a creative challenge. I should
warn you that when you first try, it seems like a great deal of work.
The only way to be successful at it is to practice, practice, practice.

Whenever I have an opportunity to make an analogy to something, I do it just for the fun of it and to keep in shape, so to speak.
The other day, for example, a friend told me about an encounter he'd
had with a grizzly in Alaska when he was a young man. He said that
many people in bear country wear bells to let the bear know they're
coming. Bears are normally shy but don't like surprises. The sound of
the bell gives them a chance to move away. It struck me immediately
that "bear bells," worn to avoid surprising a dangerous foe, are a wonderfully vivid image, ready to be used in my work as half of an effective
analogy of some kind. I've discovered that, because of practice, analogies now come quickly to my mind. Whereas before, they took a lot of
effort.

The first step is to think about the point you wish to convey. Let's
say you're trying to persuade a client not to choose an advertising
campaign that is too conservative. So you might settle on the theme
that a conservative campaign creates a bland experience for viewers,
and as a result the company's products will not stand out in the marketplace. Take that theme—"bland advertising campaigns fail to create
recognition"—and then think of as many bland experiences you can
have in life. Focus more on the personal side rather than the business
side. As you list these you'll realize rather quickly that some of these
experiences won't work at all as analogies in this case. They just don't
fit. But others do seem comparable.

Now shrink these down to the few that exactly fit your theme.
As a double check, think for a moment about the audience you'll be
addressing. Decide which of your analogy candidates would work better for these particular listeners. Which are likeliest to match their own
personal experiences? Which are likeliest to catch their interest? You
might not choose a sports analogy, for example, for a chess-playing
colleague.

The key thing is to choose one that makes the same point you
want to make, in a colorful and engaging way. Your point here is that
bland advertising can fail you in the marketplace. You want to choose
an experience about something or someone who was bland and suffering for it, and then did something lively and scored—maybe a reticent

young man you know who suddenly started getting dates with women the day he put a flower in his buttonhole. See the case described below in which Sharon found an effective analogy.

For example, you might tell a story of entering a resort hotel room where everything in the room is beige in color—the carpets, the walls, the pictures, the bedspreads, the furniture, even the television. You've paid a lot of money to have a fun-filled holiday, and now you are standing in this absolutely boring room. There's no sense of fun here. It feels like your dentist's waiting room. So you wander across the street to a nearby hotel and ask to see one of their rooms. You enter one, and the room is beautifully decorated with antiques, vibrant pastel drawings, a warm floral bedspread, elegant striped wallpaper, colorful lounge chairs. Now this is where you want to spend your vacation. The moral is: Bland advertising just isn't inviting and energizing. Nothing stands out. Better to be colorful and unique. It's the most powerful way to attract customers.

Case in Point:
How Jerry Found Compelling Evidence

Jerry was in a quandary. He had been hired by an accounting company to be its director of industry sales. He had come from a telecommunications company and was an outsider to the accounting industry. His first presentation to the organization was in a week's time. One of his top goals for this meeting was to convince the group that they could be much more visionary than they had been.

From his prior career, he had numerous examples of telecommunications companies that were truly visionary. But he worried that people in the audience might say to themselves, "Oh, it's easy for telecommunications companies to be visionary because new technologies are always appearing. But auditing and tax firms really are not often revolutionary. What this guy is saying just does not apply to us." To successfully persuade his listeners, Jerry knew that he had to find examples of farsighted companies and individuals in their own industry.

He got on the phone and called several new acquaintances in the field. Within an hour, he'd come up with a number of useful examples of visionary initiatives. He then tracked down more information on them. Then he filled his speech with convincing examples of visionary ideas and initiatives in the professional services field.

His new colleagues left the meeting impressed with Jerry's quick study of their industry as well as the sense that, as Jerry suggested, they did need to challenge their own routines and standards and become more visionary.

Case in Point:
How Sharon Developed
a Compelling Position

Sharon, the president of the division, was searching for an analogy to convince the division management that the organizational change they were planning would be a messy process with lots of unanticipated twists and turns. She felt that her managers had no idea of the unpleasant surprises they were going to encounter. As a result, they had no contingency plans. Her managers simply assumed that good planning would overcome all obstacles. Most of them had never experienced major organizational change. But Sharon had, at her previous company. She wanted her managers to be prepared and not to imagine that plans would solve everything. She wanted them flexible enough to anticipate the unexpected.

She knew that she could lecture them about this, try to reason with them, even issue warnings. But none of it would affect them as powerfully as the perfect analogy. To find it, she focused her thoughts on a very specific theme: Planning takes you only so far; you've got to expect the unexpected and be ready to adapt.

She thought about the kinds of personal experiences we all have with big change, change that *(1)* seems manageable at first but then *(2)* turns out to be unsettling and *(3)* requires us to learn new ways of doing things.

"I felt that these characteristics were the essence of what the management team needed to understand," she said. "I catalogued in my mind all the events I could think of. One was going to college for the first time. Another was learning from our first job. Another was getting married and having a baby. And there was moving to a new home. As I thought back to my audience, I realized they were older managers. Not for a long time had they gone to school, had a first job, gotten married, or had babies.

"But I knew our company often moved senior people around. A move would be the experience still fresh in their minds. I reflected on my own moves and all of their unsettling aspects. The packing and unpacking. The search for a convenient grocery store. All those change-of-address cards to mail out. I liked the theme, but *none* of these, however, had the element of unpleasant surprise I was searching for.

"I asked myself: 'What is something you think you can plan after a move, but that you can't completely?' I made a short list, and one event immediately stood out: Traveling from my new home to my new office for the first time, my first day on the job. Before heading out I always studied a map to determine the most direct route to the office. That is planning.

"Well, guess what. It rarely turns out to be the most efficient route. There are traffic jams, school zones, construction sites, and one-way streets along that direct route shown on the map. Even though it showed the way clearly, even the best map couldn't reveal unexpected outcomes. I had to discover by trial and error that what on the map seemed a longer route was usually the shorter route because there were none of the school zones and traffic tie-ups of the shorter route to slow me down."

This was the analogy that Sharon settled on to convey to her group the reality of organizational change. As they listened, she could see that it was having the impact she had hoped for.

Exhibit 7[21]
How to Size People Up by Their Myers-Briggs Type

SENSORS VS. INTUITIVES

Sensors

Does the person . . .
- like to do things in the accepted way?
- prefer realistic people?
- like people who have their feet on the ground?
- value common sense?
- prefer pragmatism and concrete experience?

Intuitives

Does the person . . .
- like to invent a way of his own?
- prefer imaginative people?
- like people who are always coming up with new ideas?
- value vision?
- prefer abstraction and theory?

THINKERS VS. FEELERS

Thinkers

Does the person . . .
- allow his head to rule his heart?
- value logic?
- have greater concern about people's rights?
- value objectivity?
- like to be firm?
- like to be seen as reasonable?

Feelers

Does the person . . .
- allow his heart to rule his head?
- value sentiment?
- have greater concern about people's feelings?

Exhibit 8[22]
How to Persuade Each Myers-Briggs Type

CONVINCING SENSORS

- Be tactful.
- Document successful applications.
- Reduce risk factors with evidence.
- Thoroughly work out details in advance.
- Show why it makes sense.

CONVINCING INTUITIVES

- Give global scheme.
- Emphasize not letting opportunity pass.
- Use confidence and enthusiasm.
- Indicate challenges.
- Point out future benefits.

CONVINCING THINKERS

- Be logical.
- State the principles involved.
- Stress competent handling of issue.
- Be logical in presenting points.
- Clearly list costs and benefits.

CONVINCING FEELERS

- Tell who else is for the idea.
- Be personable and friendly.
- Indicate how it's helpful.

6
Connecting
Emotionally

Connecting emotionally with our colleagues is crucial to persuasion. Actors' performances are most powerful and effective when in our eyes they are emotionally the characters they're playing. It's the same for the rest of us. We can have credibility in our persuasion, and an effective frame and good supporting evidence, but if we lack emotional connection to our position, then colleagues will sense it. They'll wonder if it signals doubt or uncertainty or manipulation. Then the degree of perceived risk in supporting us skyrockets.

In research that I have conducted on business leaders, I found that the most effective leaders draw upon their emotions to generate commitment. They understand that the heart and the soul are often far more potent energizers than the head. Aristotle himself believed strongly in the emotional engagement of an audience as a critical factor in persuasion. A persuader's appeal must convey his own commitment and touch a chord of feelings with his audience. We can accomplish this by sharing sincere feelings that mirror the desires, needs, hopes, fears, dreams, and values of those whom we are persuading.

Think of emotions as interpretations made by ourselves and our colleagues about something or someone. For example, I *feel* happy on a sunny day. Or I *feel* depressed on a rainy day. Or I *feel* proud when our team launches an innovative product that is a market success. Or I *feel* anxious when the competition lowers their prices. If the conditions are like X, then I feel like Y.[1]

If we wish to use emotions in our persuasive appeals, we have to focus on the personal experiences of our audiences and ask ourselves how they are most likely to *interpret* the positions we offer them. If X happens, how are my colleagues likely to feel? The key to tapping the emotions is to engage our colleagues, as always, in terms of their own experiences. We must be careful not to assume that what we feel emotionally about our position will always be the same as what our audience feels.

A nice actual example of one such mismatch involves a company president who was attempting to motivate his senior management team into a greater sense of urgency about the company's future. He assumed *his* emotional reactions about the future would be shared by his audience. As a result, his approach backfired. Here is what happened.

One afternoon the president called his management team together into the boardroom. As the executives entered, they saw an overhead transparency showing a smiling man who was flying an old-fashioned biplane, scarf blowing in the wind. The right half of the transparency was covered. When everyone was assembled, the president greeted the group and explained that he was feeling like this little pilot given the company's recent good fortunes. They had just finished their most successful year in history—both sales and profits were way up. Then he paused.

With a sigh, he started again. His happiness was quickly disappearing, he said. Partly lifting the paper sheet covering the other half of the overhead, he revealed a new image of the pilot. He was still flying, but this time his smile had become a frown. As the president raised the remaining portion of the sheet, it became apparent that the pilot was now flying directly at a wall. Everyone suddenly realized that the little pilot was about to crash!

Like this new image of the pilot, the president was now frowning. He faced his audience and with a heavy voice said, "I'm

very unhappy today because this is what I see happening to us."
He went on to criticize the group for not being concerned about
the company's future. The company was headed for a crash, he
warned, if people didn't take action fast.

Minutes after the meeting ended, managers gathered in small
groups in the hallways to discuss the president's "scare tactic," as it
quickly came to be called. Instead of reacting with constructive
concern, they resented the president's clumsy attempt at emotional
manipulation. Why, exactly?

For one thing, the management team felt that the president
was out of touch with *their* emotions. The managers had gone into
that meeting feeling proud of their successful year. Every one of
them believed they were working harder and smarter than ever
before, and that they well understood the challenges the future
posed. Yet the president didn't congratulate them on their performance. Instead of praising them he slapped them for not doing
enough.

The feelings of blame and scolding that the president had
chosen to convey in his presentation were out of sync with the
expectations of his management team. He not only failed to persuade them but also harmed his own image.

What might he have done instead? First, he should have held
a separate session devoted simply to celebrating and praising the
team's accomplishments. Then later, in a second meeting, he could
have surfaced his own anxieties. Also, rather than blaming the
team for ignoring the future, he should have calmly described
what he saw as emerging threats to the company, then asked the
managers to help him develop new initiatives.

Contrast that story with this one:[2]

Orit Gadiesh, vice chairman of Bain & Co., a well-known
Boston consulting firm, found herself debating what to say to company employees who would be attending the company's August
1992 annual meeting at Waterville Valley, New Hampshire, the
following week.

Founded in 1973, Bain & Co. had grown rapidly, increasing
revenues by as much as 50 percent a year, from approximately
$750,000 in 1975 to $175 million worldwide by 1991.[3] The number of consultants and staff had grown as well, reaching six hun-

dred in 1991.[4] Between 1985 and 1989, Bain & Co.'s phenomenal growth rate outperformed the average growth rate for consulting firms—15 percent a year—by a large margin.[5]

After more than a decade of outstanding growth, however, the company hit a bump. Founder Bill Bain and his original partners decided the time was right to harvest the rewards of their labors. In 1985 and 1986, in two transactions, the seven founding partners of the company plus one other partner sold 30 percent of the company to create an ESOP (employee stock ownership plan). The eight partners received a total of approximately $200 million in notes and in cash, which the company had to borrow. The firm was left with $25 million a year in interest payments, to be paid out of its future revenues.

Not only was the company burdened with big debt but the valuation of Bain & Co. reportedly became controversial. The valuation was based upon estimates of exponentially increasing future revenues and profits. While Bain & Co.'s profitability did continue to grow, it did not do so exponentially, and interest expenses began to demand the lion's share of the profits.

What's more, competition from an increasing number of "boutique" strategy consultants intensified.[6] In 1988, as interest payments soared, Bain had to lay off 10 percent of its consultants, most of whom were higher-level, longtime employees. These were the first layoffs in the firm's history and were seen as "a breach of the social contract."[7] Morale plummeted.

In January of 1991, a compromise was reached with the founders. They agreed in effect to return approximately $100 million to the firm in cash and forgiven debt and give the remaining 70 percent of the stock to the company.

Things promptly began to improve. By 1992 the company's revenues and profits had climbed to pre-1990 levels. A renewed sense of direction emerged within the leadership of the firm.

In the spring of 1992, a year and a half into the transition, Orit Gadiesh began to focus on the task of reviving a collective sense of pride and confidence in the company. One evening at dinner with a professor from the Harvard Business School, she was asked what she liked most about her work. She responded that she most liked "being a part of an exceptional organization that always rises to the challenge and does the impossible in everything we put our minds to." He commented that it seemed an amazing response considering what Bain had just gone through. Orit instantly replied: "That's the most frustrating thing! What we've gone through [internally], while distracting on many dimensions, hasn't changed the quality of what we're doing, and it doesn't keep me from feeling proud of our work."

Later she reflected on that fervent response to the professor's question: "I had to think about why I reacted so quickly and it began to dawn on me that I had never lost my pride in what we were doing. By pride I meant a conviction that what Bain & Co. had set out to do was really worth doing, a conviction that enough of us were still passionate about what we did. This shared passion was what had once made this place great. I was sure we could do it again."

As she prepared her speech for the company's annual meeting, she began to think about how to address this issue of pride. She knew she needed to rekindle the organization's collective pride, but how? How could she persuade the organization to have pride again?

She began with private discussions with several trusted colleagues, asking each of them how the staff might react to a very personal speech. When she approached Jon Mark, a director at the firm, he discouraged her from giving a "from the heart" sort of pitch:

> Don't tell the people at Bain & Co. what they should believe in. Give them facts and data and let them draw their own conclusions. If pride is the outcome of giving them the facts and data, that's great, but don't tell people that they need to turn around their pride.
>
> First of all, they don't like to be told what to do, and second, you would be telling them they don't have a lot of pride now, which I don't think is necessarily good. Just put the data on the table and have that inexorable build-up of data lead them to the inevitable conclusion —which would be pride. Don't stand up there and say, "Now is the time to be proud."

Mark felt that Orit had only a 50 percent chance of succeeding with an emotional speech. He even offered to help her draft a speech consisting of statistics and charts that would illustrate how well the company had done in the past year.

Orit had worked closely with Mark for over a decade and had tremendous respect for his opinion. She knew that people at Bain tended to be independent, self-motivated personalities. They might not like an emotional approach to the issue. History had shown that analytical speeches usually worked well in the firm, while emotional ones without charts and graphs were treated with suspicion. In addition, Orit was concerned that trying to capture such intangible issues as collective pride and renewed spirit at Bain & Co. in a forty-minute speech would come off sounding too simplistic.

Now in doubt about a "from the heart" speech, she approached David Harding, a vice president and another longtime colleague. Harding felt she should give a more personal speech— one that would match both Orit's and the organization's actual moods. While he acknowledged that "the culture here decidedly leans towards the rational approach to things," he strongly believed that "people in the company needed to be congratulated for coming through an extraordinary time in the company's history together. But there's a stoicism which prevents people from being comfortable in saying that.

"It's important to take the time out to congratulate the people in the room on a job well done," Harding said emphatically. "You need to say these things, people really need to hear them." A "numbers" speech, he added, would instead connect pride to how much the company had grown or earned, rather than to the company's values, its team, and every individual consultant.

After weeks of debate, Orit finally decided on the more personal, "no numbers" speech. Standing at the podium, Orit Gadiesh, vice chairman of Bain & Co., drew a very deep breath. As she peered out over the members of the audience, she felt her resolve grow. She opened with a joke to break the ice, then began her speech:

> I want to talk to you today about confidence and
> pride in what we do. I know this sounds a little strange,

but bear with me for a moment. Let me give you a sense of where this comes from.

A couple of months ago, I had dinner with a business-school professor who is a friend of mine. In the course of the dinner, somewhat to my surprise, he asked me what I liked the most about what I do, and what I found most frustrating. The answer to the first part came easily, and I can summarize it here in one sentence: What I love most about my work is the fact that I am part of a team that produces the most extraordinary work, and continuously beats the odds and does the impossible in everything we put our minds to. I really believe it.

"Gee," he said, "that's an awful lot of self-confidence from someone who has just gone through what you all have. . . ."

"That," I said, "is my biggest frustration—the fact that some people actually believe that the last year and a half—while distracting on many dimensions—would distract us from doing what we do best, or from feeling very proud about it."

My answer was so instantaneous, so much from the gut, that I actually had to stop and think about it: What *did* I mean when I said pride?

I realized that by pride I meant a conviction that what Bain & Co. set out to do was worth doing. And that for a year and a half, many of us believed that if we could just cut through all the bull, we would get back to it. A conviction that enough of us were still passionate about what we do, and that shared passion was what had made this place great. And that we could do it again. In fact, that was precisely what carried us through what were undeniably hard times.

My friend the professor was startled. "Wow," he said. "If enough people feel like you do, Bain & Co. is going to be truly unstoppable."

I've been thinking about this ever since. I guess we stopped projecting self confidence . . . [but] I think very few—if any—of us ever really lost our pride in what we were doing individually in our work. But for a while there, we lost our *collective* pride. . . . That thought kept bugging me. There is a fine line between arrogance and pride, and believe me, we've crossed that line in the past. But, boy was it powerful when we stayed on the right side of this line and projected it!

I talked about it with a number of you. People got it. It was hard to put a finger on what it meant, but it resonated. . . . We really have turned around everywhere our competitors said we would not be able to: We've turned around financially, and we've turned around the business—and even our competitors are beginning to acknowledge that. Now it's time to turn around what they really fear, what they have always envied us for, what made them the most uneasy—as crazy as this sounds: It's time to turn around our collective pride in what we do!

Orit continued to talk for thirty-five minutes, concentrating on the accomplishments of the past year. She related anecdotes that illustrated how impressive the work of the various teams had been and how much clients had deeply appreciated their efforts. In one example, she shared a letter written by the division president of a large financial services company, which was addressed to every member of the team, complimenting them on their outstanding work. She stressed how these examples had come from all levels of the organization and that cumulatively these instances and many others like them were having an impact on the building of powerful relationships with clients. With a few minutes remaining, she concluded:

I've asked you to listen to what people say about the power of what you do. I've asked you to look at each other and not take for granted what others envy us for. Our clients don't—they love it! Our competitors don't—they fear it! It's time for us to project it again: Internally among ourselves because we will have more fun, and externally to the world.

Each and every one of us is an ambassador of our

company. Each and every one of us is part of the team. Whether you are in the administrative staff convincing someone to apply for a job, or helping a colleague get through a bad day. Whether you are a consultant or an associate consultant, striking up a conversation on a plane or celebrating your friends' successes in your area. Whether you are talking to a potential employee or client, or working with your team—who you are and what you believe comes through. You can only say what you believe. You can only project what you feel. That's all I ask.

I told you how I feel. I told you why I'm proud. I hope you share some of it. Because when we believe in ourselves the way others do, our turnaround will be complete. And when we collectively project it, we are— as my friend the professor said—truly unstoppable.

As Orit finished, there was a moment of silence, then suddenly thunderous applause. One vice president was so moved by the speech that while everyone was applauding, he walked up to the front of the room, shook Orit's hand, and thanked her.

Over the coming months, staff members would recall that moment as the point when pride had come back to the firm. In meetings myself with Bain consultants several months after the speech, I heard time after time again how Orit's emotional commitment in that speech had restored faith in the firm and persuaded employees that they were back on the road to greatness.

Why was Orit's presentation so effective in motivating the group into a new state of mind?

First, her words became a symbol of the organization's regaining the spirit that once had existed at Bain. The company historically had been characterized by a very strong culture of camaraderie and pride. These were the feelings that her colleagues were longing to restore. But the duration of the downsizing trauma had weakened self-confidence despite new successes. What Orit did was to say that *now* is the time: We are already back to our former greatness. She crystallized the moment: We no longer need to be in doubt.

What she had done was to align her persuasion exactly to the emotional state of her audience. She could do that so perfectly because it was her own true state as well.

She knew that her people were emotionally longing for security and a sense of momentum, eager to believe that the firm was no longer in trouble and that it would continue to be a major force in its industry. Orit's recounting of recent success stories, her use of the letter of praise written by the executive of the financial services company—both spoke to this longing and eagerness. They were also powerful evidence.

If Orit had simply stated that the firm needed to regain its pride, it wouldn't have been effective. It would have been like telling someone to love you; feelings can't be commanded, they have to be experienced. If Orit had said, "I want all of us to feel more pride in what we do," this would have been interpreted as a command. Immediately the audience would have resisted, especially those independent and critically minded consultants. Instead, the stories, like courtroom testimony, provided evidence to an audience of consultants who needed proofs.

She also used an outside expert—the business school professor—to draw the conclusion she wanted them to reach: that Bain would become truly unstoppable. Here she implicitly and successfully conveyed the assumption that if an outside, credible expert saw the link, then there must be something to it. The comment he made, "If enough people feel like you do . . . ," gave authority to Orit's thesis that if all Bain employees felt pride as intensely as Orit did, then they as a firm would regain their former greatness. It was within their grasp, and greater pride had become the essential turnaround ingredient.

Orit framed the pride issue initially in terms of a personal experience, a dinner conversation. By means of the story of the revelation she had at that dinner, she made it possible for each member of the audience to have a similar revelation—an awakening of his own individual pride in the organization. At the moment of her speech, she became the dinner-partner professor for her organization. Her demonstration "on stage" of her own pride in very sincere emotions became the model of company pride "refound."

Finally, Orit delivered her speech with strong emotion. It conveyed her confidence and pride in the team. The audience could feel Orit's belief in them. Her sincerity and conviction led her audience to feel that maybe, just maybe, they really were once again truly unstoppable.

Orit's speech is an example of using positive feelings to influence. But it is also possible to use emotions based upon anxiety and urgency to motivate and persuade. For example, we might portray the present situation of our organization as intolerable and highly threatening and then offer attractive future scenarios. A sense of urgency can become a powerful motivator to action, as long as it's *believable.*

Jack Welch, CEO of General Electric, has been very effective at creating a sense of urgency by posing fierce competitive scenarios, ones that demand an immediate response from company divisions (see Exhibit 1).

Robert P. Marcell, the head of Chrysler's small-car design team, pulled off a particularly impressive demonstration of this approach. In July of 1990, his team was at an impasse. The design function at Chrysler had just been divided between two groups— one for small cars and one for larger automobile models, including minivans. The small-car group felt like the company's stepchild. The vans and larger cars were the company's bread and butter. Chrysler hadn't brought out a new subcompact since 1978, the year of the Omni and the Horizon, and there was considerable feeling within the company that it should look outside for design and production of the next small car.

Negotiations to partner with Fiat were already underway, and more talks had been held with Hyundai and another Asian manufacturer. Iacocca himself strongly preferred an arrangement outside Chrysler, to minimize the risk and to protect the company's cash position. Marcell's daunting task was to convince himself, his employees, and ultimately Iacocca to give his group a chance. At the time, this chance looked close to zero. But Marcell is a persistent fighter:

> I knew that if I didn't take this risk, we wouldn't do the car. I had one thousand people in my group. Their jobs, their management positions, were at stake. I

wanted them to see the real mission that we were on. To go on the offensive. To launch a counterattack. I wanted them to see that we could build a small car ourselves. I sensed that the way we could do it was through team-work and daring to be different in almost everything we did.

Marcell decided to call a town meeting of his staff. His chal-lenge was to convince his somewhat demoralized team that they could design an excellent small car. He could, for instance, tell them simply to work harder on the project. Or he could scare them with the possibility of job cuts. But he decided not to do either.

I didn't want people stewing on the question "Do we have a job today?" I also believe you can't just go out and tell people they're empowered. I wanted instead to allay their fears. I wanted a more proactive approach. I knew that if I could appeal to their hearts, they'd act.

I decided to show them how my hometown had been decimated by outside competition . . . but at the same time show them my belief in their ability to create a great small car.

He prepared a fifteen-minute talk based on slides of current scenes from his hometown, Iron River, a now-defunct mining town in upper Michigan. Up onto the screen flashed photographs he had taken of his boarded-up high school, the shuttered homes of his childhood friends, the crumbling ruins of the town iron works, the closed churches, and the abandoned rail yard where a thousand freight cars used to gather daily. After his emotional description of each of these places, he said the words, "We couldn't compete," like the refrain of a hymn.

Marcell implied that the same outcome awaited Detroit and that terminating the production of small cars would only accelerate the process. But if Chrysler could somehow build a profitable sub-compact, it might just reverse that whole trend.

He closed his talk by challenging the team to build a "made-in-America" subcompact that would prove that Chrysler—and America—could compete.

It was the most emotional speech of Marcell's career. The impact was immediate. "You could feel the energy in the room," Marcell told me. "And for the following week, I had dozens of phone calls—thanking me, saying how moved they were."

His team was now ready to tackle mountains. He had used fear in a constructive manner by linking the desolation of the American enterprise system to the devastation of his home community. Behind this message, however, was one of hope that drew on the deep, common belief that Americans can overcome difficult odds and triumph. It was a perfect example of framing issues around shared values. It mirrored the feelings of his audience, longing to lift themselves and the nation out of their troubles.

Marcell took this slide show to Chrysler's senior executives and ultimately to Lee Iacocca. Before his session with Iacocca he was informed that Iacocca could give him just twenty minutes, and that he'd probably not have positive news for Marcell at the end of it.

During the meeting, as Marcell moved through his slides, he could see that Iacocca was touched. Marcell's presentation was not too different from Iacocca's earlier appeal to Congress to save Chrysler itself.

At the end of his show, Marcell stopped and said, "If we dare to be different, we could be the reason the U.S. auto industry survives. We could be the reason our kids and grand-kids don't end up in fast-food service." Iacocca stayed on for a total of two hours as Marcell explained in greater detail what his team was planning. Soon afterward Iacocca changed his mind and gave Marcell's group approval to develop a car, the Neon.

In September 1993, the new subcompact was given its debut at the Frankfurt auto show. Production began in January of 1994 for the U.S. and four months later in Europe. Bob Marcell's persuasion had turned an idea into a reality in three and a half years. *Business Week* would exclaim: "With a base price of $8,600, the Neon could just beat the Japanese at their game of selling well-equipped small cars at a profit."[8] And so it did, reviving a Chrysler division and saving thousands of jobs.

To persuade, Marcell had used a simple logic based on a vivid, alarming example, then a shot of optimism: "We can do it. We have the power within ourselves." Along with Orit Gadiesh's presentation, it was one of the most inspired uses of emotion to influence an audience that I have seen in the world of business.

You might be asking yourself at this point in the discussion, "But can I really bring myself to use anxiety and fear as a motivator?" Many of us recall our drivers' education course in high school where we were shown gory accident scenes to "persuade" us to drive carefully. It is commonplace to hear company executives, in the great old drivers'-ed tradition, using heavy-handed scare tactics to encourage more rapid change in their organizations. *Fortune* magazine even had a recent article entitled, "Times are Good? Create a Crisis." But are such approaches as effective as the constructive ones like Bob Marcell's?

Research on the use of fear suggests that it is extremely difficult to actually manipulate the level of fear experienced by an audience. We saw this with our opening example of the company president and his presentation with the little pilot. Managers who try are likely to have hit-and-miss results. We could include in a message all sorts of elements that seem scary to us but might have little effect on our colleagues. One social scientist whose specialty is persuasion comments: "Even experienced researchers working with carefully controlled experimental materials have found it difficult to induce the intended degrees of fear dependably."[9]

Research also indicates that when a message does succeed at inducing fear or anxiety it can indeed increase its persuasiveness, as we saw with the Marcell example. When listeners feel greater fear following a persuasive message, they are generally more persuaded. So using fear to persuade is a bit of a catch-22. Messages that do arouse greater anxiety are more persuasive, but the problem is that shaping these messages effectively is extremely difficult to do.

Sometimes a more toned-down version of the implications of a crisis may be more persuasive, simply because it will appear less exaggerated and therefore more believable.[10]

• • •

As we have seen over the last four chapters, there are certain essential ingredients to constructive persuasion. Employing these approaches effectively can significantly enhance our ability to garner commitment to solutions. They are quite different from our older stereotypes of persuasion as a largely self-serving tool. Instead, the new models of persuasion offer us tools we need to be the leaders of the peer-based organizations of the twenty-first century.

Constructive persuasion must be backed up by action. In our concluding chapter, we see how, for truly effective leadership, our persuasion and our actions must go hand-in-hand.

Exhibit 1

An Excerpt from Jack Welch's Speech to General Electric's 1989 Annual Shareholders Meeting

"It's time to look at the '90's, and it is not a view for the faint of heart . . . For the environment and the events we see rushing toward us make the tough, tumultuous '80's look like a decade at the beach.

"Ahead of us are Darwinian shakeouts in every major marketplace, with no consolation prizes for the losing companies and nations.

"Our view as we entered the '80's focused, appropriately, on one powerful competitor: Japan, Inc. As we stand on the threshold of the '90's, we face not only an even more powerful Japan but a revitalized, confident Europe moving closer together and led by bold, aggressive entrepreneurs of a kind we simply didn't encounter in the '70's or early '80's.

"At the beginning of the '80's, Korea and Taiwan were principally sourcing centers for labor-intensive electronic products. They enter the '90's as innovative manufacturing powerhouses challenging the world in electronics, autos, steel and a dozen other industries. Behind them on the same path come the other nations of the Far East including a potential colossus of the next century

. . . China. The global market pie is not growing at nearly the rate necessary to satisfy the hunger of those after it.

"In the '80's, GE built its businesses on a foundation of quality, technology, marketing and sustained investment. Internal growth plus a successful series of acquisitions were sufficient to propel us to world leadership in each of our 14 [business groups]. But simply doing more of what worked in the '80's will not be enough to win in the '90's when the indispensable additional ingredient will be speed: getting there faster . . . getting there first." [11]

Practice Session: How to Put Emotion to Work for You

In the business world, we like to imagine that our colleagues make their decisions rationally, yet if we scratch beneath the surface we will always find emotions at play. Our task as effective persuaders is to speak these emotions in ways that link them to our position.

A warning is in order, however: Relying on emotions alone to convince others will cause your listener to feel manipulated or give him the impression you act without thinking. You must always have a foundation of good reasons and evidence underpinning your emotional appeals. Without them, your arguments will seem unfounded.

I'll give you an analogy to show you what I mean. In wine making you need good grapes, the right soil, and perfect fermentation. These elements are like your supporting evidence. But there are other, subjective factors that influence a person's response to a wine: its color, the beauty of its label, the shape of its bottle, and the mystique the vintner has managed to create for it. The wine is the wine, no matter what the esthetics, but the esthetics touch on our feelings and add to the experience of drinking it. Similarly, the right emotional appeal, added to your evidence, can enhance the reception your listeners give your positions.

Emotions can also reveal our own commitment to the position we are arguing. They can indicate which aspects of our positions need work in order to become more convincing.

Exercise One: Are You Ready to Convince?

Start by asking yourself very candidly: "How do I feel emotionally about what I am about to persuade? Am I excited about it, enthusiastic? How will its successful outcomes make me feel? Proud? Powerful? Full of satisfaction?"

Note down the two or three major emotional responses you've identified.

If you find that your feelings are uncertain and ambivalent, then you know something's amiss. Ambivalence is the red warning light on the dashboard of our persuasion. It tells us it's time to pull over and look under the hood. You'll remember that early in the book I mentioned that good persuaders arrive at their position only after a good bit of self-convincing—after studying the important facts and talking to others who have some expertise. If you're ambivalent, you're probably not at this stage yet. If you go out to persuade while still ambivalent, you'll reveal your self-doubt and undermine your ability to persuade effectively.

If you're in this state, go back to the drawing board. Do more research and involve more experts until you get greater clarity. Or find compromises that make sense and clear up your ambivalence.

Exercise Two:
Matching Your Emotions with Theirs

Let's say you're fairly well convinced. Mentally, go around the imaginary table of colleagues you need to persuade. Ask yourself: "What will this person's emotional reaction be to my initiative?" If you predict a person's feelings will be neutral or negative, you're in a weak position with him. If, however, his predicted feelings fit with your own, he'll feel enthusiastic, for example, just as you do; then you need to ensure that you convey those shared feelings clearly as you state your position. What we want in effective persuasion is a powerful overlap of feelings about an issue.

Exercise Three:
Finding Emotion-Generating Material

Think of values, examples, company stories, and analogies that you believe will have emotional appeal for each of your colleagues. Think of Robert Marcell of Chrysler, who tied his pitch for the Neon to the devastation of his hometown. Think of Orit Gadiesh of Bain & Co., who told her listeners about the professor who could see Bain's enormous potential. Ask yourself what experiences you could convey that would have strong emotional appeal for your colleagues. Use them liberally throughout your presentation.

But remember, they must be events they can relate to and which, for them, have the same emotional significance as they do for you.

Exercise Four:
Checking Your Evidence for
Emotional Implications

Walk yourself through your supporting evidence to see how each of your colleagues might react to it. To you, the project may seem an exciting new entrepreneurial venture; for one of your listeners, however, it may look like a high-risk investment. That person doesn't feel enthusiasm, he feels anxiety. Your position and evidence must first address that anxiety.

To get at the feelings of someone like that you need to identify what aspects of the project trigger his negative emotions. Then you must tailor your evidence very carefully, so that it converts the negative to a positive or, at the least, a neutral.

Say he's anxious about the downside risk of your idea. You'd want to show him how you've covered it, so that there's actually limited risk.

In short, we have to understand each colleague's core emotional reaction and then tailor our frames and evidence to reinforce their positive emotions and neutralize their negative reactions.

Exercise Five: Anticipating Trouble

If you believe your audience will react at first with skepticism, prepare yourself to say something like this: "I know that some of us might feel a bit skeptical about this initiative. It does have its limitations. . . ."

Then mention the limitations you know they're thinking of.

Then go on to say, "But here is why it may have potential. . . ."

One Final Caution

Don't try to act out emotions. Leave that to professional actors. It's best to be sincere, never to fake it. If you don't have the emotion yourself, don't try to manufacture it.

Case in Point: How Gretchen Did Her Emotional Homework

Gretchen, the senior new products director, was eager to build support for a new line of toys. She could hardly contain her enthusiasm for the early designs she'd seen from the development group. The company had been gradually losing market share for some time and needed fresh new products. Its last big hit was three years before.

Gretchen ran an internal check of her own emotions about what she was going to persuade. She realized that the pricing of the new line was the one area where she was still not convinced. She could feel her own ambivalence. She decided to take an extra week before setting up a meeting with the key decision makers. She spent that week working out different pricing scenarios with two colleagues, one a guru in marketing, the other a financial analyst. After a great deal of study she finally identified a pricing range she felt confident about. Now she was ready to persuade.

The key decision makers were all top executives of the company. She carefully assessed each person's probable emotional reactions to the new product line.

She recalled the marketing VP's reaction when he caught a glimpse of one of the sketches. He raved on and on about it for ten minutes. He had a passion for beautiful design and said this was one of the best he'd seen. He was, in short, already emotionally bonded to the product.

The sales VP, Debbie, was in a desperate state. She could see the erosion of the company's strength daily in the marketplace. Her prime feeling would probably be anxiety. Gretchen knew that the sales projections she had calculated with her marketing colleague would have the greatest emotional appeal for Debbie. They'd offer her a sense of hope: The conservative estimates showed double-digit growth over the next four years.

The manufacturing VP and the chief financial officer both believed that cost containment and better distribution were the keys to solving the company's problems. Investments in new products were lower on their list of priorities. Their support, however, was crucial if she was to get the sizable investments needed to launch an entirely new line.

As she reflected on how to pitch her appeal, she focused on the emotional concerns of the VP and the CFO, their strong concern about the company's future well-being. They were old-timers and very loyal to the firm. Both had been with the firm since its very beginnings, a turbulent time when the company's first real break came with the founder's high stakes gamble on a single new toy. How could she speak to those experiences and longtime loyalties?

She had a member of the engineering staff run a series of estimates on production costs. He showed her that a few small, clever changes in design and materials would reduce the estimates by 30 percent without changing the toy overall. These refinements would actually make the new line one of the company's least expensive to manufacture. She decided to present this evidence early on to address the anxiety of the manufacturing VP and the CFO about new investment levels.

Russ, the company president, had been intimately involved with the design team. He was a former designer himself, and the new toys were his favorites to date. He believed in Gretchen's business sense, and her enthusiasm seemed to confirm his intuition about the new designs.

In the meeting, Gretchen's retelling of the tale about the founder's brave and successful gamble along with her sound cost projections, moved the CFO and VP of manufacturing. Then Russ weighed in and took them the rest of the way to full support. There were no nasty surprises. Everything fell into place. Gretchen had correctly assessed the emotional predisposition of each person in the room.

7 The Persuasion Power Boost: Actions

We've been exploring the verbal skills it takes to persuade well. But there's more to persuasion than just talking—namely, actions. If we can reinforce our arguments with actions, we can powerfully boost the persuasive appeal of our words. It's a twist on the old saying: Actions and words speak louder together than alone.

To show you how this works, I'm going to tell you the remarkable story of Jim Dawson and his company, Zebco. It's a classic case of a manager who used actions to power his persuasion. Along the way it illustrates many of the persuasion principles we've discussed in this book.

The Zebco Story: Early History

To set the stage for the persuasion challenge facing Jim, we have to go back a bit to the origins of Zebco, a company that was, oddly enough, enjoying too much success when he arrived.

Zebco had a peculiar beginning some 45 years before, when a

watchmaker from west Texas was buying some meat for the family table. The watchmaker, R.D. Hull, was a passionate fisherman, and like most fishermen of his time he'd had trouble with his baitcast fishing line. It was always snarling in the reel. One day he went to his neighborhood grocery and ordered a steak. He watched as the clerk wrapped it, pulling string from a large spool attached to the counter. A light bulb lit in R.D.'s head. This stationary spool inspired him to invent a casting reel that would not snarl or backlash.

He then looked for a company to manufacture it. On his list was the Zero Hour Bomb Company, an oil-field equipment firm in Tulsa, Oklahoma. It made electric time bombs for oil well drilling. R.D. arrived holding a strange device in his hand. It looked like a tin can with a hole in either end.

The company's executives found R.D.'s idea intriguing and agreed to build and market his fishing reel under the name of Zebco, the acronym for Zero Hour Bomb Company. In June of 1949, on the first day of production, twenty-five handmade Zebco Standards were produced.

The timing couldn't have been better. The market for electric time bombs would soon disappear, and the Zero Hour Bomb Company would transform itself into the Zebco fishing reel company. R.D.'s reel was only the beginning of the company's fishing innovations. In 1960, it developed what it called "balanced tackle," with the rod, reel, and line functioning smoothly as a single unit. The next year the result, the Zebco 202, appeared. It went on to break fishing history, selling over 62 million and becoming the largest selling reel in the world.

Thanks to its innovative products and the explosive growth in the popularity of sport fishing, Zebco would grow almost ten times in size up through the early 1980s. But trouble soon struck. In the 1970s, reels imported from Asia began to appear and in a short time were flooding the market. The Japanese had learned how to manufacture spinning reels that were not only less expensive but more beautiful, silky smooth in their operation, and technically appealing.

All the while, inflation was driving up Zebco's production costs. Rather than address the problem of high costs head-on, Zebco simply passed its increases to the customer in higher retail prices, ignoring the threat of Asian reels. It also ignored the fact that its quality, in contrast to that of many of its competitors, was relatively poor.

Inside Zebco, the workforce grew lax and uncooperative. They unionized and had their first-ever strike. Management, more interested in its perks rather than performance, grew self-indulgent. For Zebco executives, lulled by the company's success, the place became a country club. Despite the looming threats, there was no sense of urgency.

However, the parent company, the Brunswick Corporation, sensed problems at Zebco and in 1976 promoted Zebco's marketing vice president to be its president. Attuned to the changing marketplace, he held employee forums to expose the company's problems. He learned that suppliers were delivering poorly made parts that fouled up production. Resolving to blast Zebco out of its smugness and build a more competitive organization, he laid the foundation for the company's first total quality program. In 1981 he brought Jim Dawson on board as senior vice president of operations. Jim had been doing a great job running manufacturing at another Brunswick firm.

On his arrival, Jim was struck immediately by the company's complacency about costs and competition and by the workers' lack of discipline. Clearly there was a screaming need for major change.

Jim knew that his turnaround plans would go nowhere unless the entire Zebco staff agreed that change was necessary. Before he could persuade them of that fact, he would have to boost his *credibility* with the employees to get them to trust him and believe that he cared about them. Jim was at our first step of effective persuasion.

Jim's First Persuasion Mission: He Was Trustworthy and Cared About the Employees

If you think back to the chapter on building credibility, you'll remember that two dimensions are always involved in building it—expertise and relationships. Expertise was not Jim's problem. When he came to Zebco, he brought with him a strong reputation for having turned around another Brunswick division. His problem was relationship credibility. Coming from the outside, he had no existing relationships with anyone at Zebco.

He had a second relationship problem: He represented management. That was a big minus among the workforce, which had grown to distrust senior managers. Many workers believed he'd come to close down the plant.

Jim knew he had to erase this trust gap. Only highly motivated and committed employees could bring off the turnaround he envisioned. After all, he'd be asking them to make significant investments in time and energy. Without deep trust in Jim, they'd scoff at his plans.

He had to convince them that he was different from those other managers. He had to get them to believe him when he said he wasn't there to shut down the company's principal operations in Tulsa. He had to persuade them that by following Jim Dawson they could make their jobs secure and prosper.

It couldn't be done just with words. To prove himself worthy of trust, he had to *act*. He had to demonstrate that employees and management shared the same destiny, that neither side was going to benefit without the other.

He started by shattering the class differences that had grown up between management and the workforce. "Very few people understand the damage it does when you set up different classes of people," Jim explained to me. "I wanted to eliminate all the barriers between people and things that create classes of people. Once you break these down, you start this chain reaction. People start to feel a little more comfortable in facing issues, in bringing issues up. We were really working on trust factors in the beginning, building a new trust in the company especially at the bottom of the organization.

"It is so important to understand that the people at the bottom see the need for change. They see what is actually happening that should not be happening. The people at the top are protected from it. Very few people understand workforces and what turns them on and what turns them off, how you can create openness, and the fact that generally people are afraid to talk to people about unpleasant things. They also want total honesty and clarity from people at the top."

Jim began by challenging the Zebco class system at its most visible: the parking spaces reserved for senior managers. They were right at the main entrance, and each had a senior manager's name posted on it. Their message was implicit: "We're better than you are."

Late one afternoon Jim spoke one-on-one with a group of company secretaries. He told them to arrive at 7:30 the next morning, remove all the reserved parking signs, and then park their cars in the reserved spaces. When the senior managers arrived at 8:00 A.M., there would be no open spaces. Delighted, the secretaries all arrived early and filled up the spaces.

On that day, reserved parking became a program called the President's Club. Those special spaces were now for anyone who had 100 percent attendance—lineworker or manager. Jim had turned what had been a status symbol into a motivational program for everyone.

Jim then decided to remove time clocks from the factory. He felt that these were simply another barrier between the managers and the employees. They starkly signified a lack of trust. So one morning he acted again: He arrived at the bank of time clocks with a crowbar and began ripping them off the walls. Soon workers were coming from all over the company to see the amazing sight: the broken time clocks heaped on the floor, the snapped electrical conduits dangling from the wall, the unpainted silhouettes on the wall where the time clocks had been.

Jim's actions spoke far louder than his words ever could have, and the message was quite simple: We trust you to be on time and to be responsible for your hours. You will be treated no differently than our managers.

Jim took the process a step further. He role-modeled new standards for his management team. As one executive explained to me: "What we realized was that it wasn't just Jim but we managers who had to make sure that people could *see* there were no double standards. As a manager, I often work long hours. It's not unusual to work ten hours a day. I often go home at 7:00 P.M. Now the clerical and line staff don't *see* that we are here until seven because they are here only until 4:45 P.M. We managers had allowed ourselves to use that as an excuse: 'Well, I am going to come in a little late tomorrow because I stayed in the office until eight o'clock last night.' The trouble with that is that it appears to the workforce that you have a double standard. An hourly person out on the line cannot come in at 7:05 A.M. He has got to be in here at 7:00 A.M. So we realized we had to be here at the same time they did."

These dramatic actions quickly built up Jim's relationship credibility with the workforce. They would have walked through fire for him. He had demonstrated he really did care about equality in the plant and was willing to forego his own perks, including his convenient reserved parking space. It was visible proof of what he was persuading. Earlier in the book, I talked about using evidence to persuade. Jim's actions were his evidence. He was truly credible.

Building Support for His Frame: "Zebco Is in Trouble"

His credibility established, Jim set out to persuade the organization that Zebco was in big trouble and that urgent attention was needed. His persuasion task was formidable. How would he ever convince a successful and still growing company that it was headed for disaster?

In chapter 6 we talked about the role of framing in persuasion, and of framing's connection to positions and evidence. Jim's frame in this case was the following:

"Despite its success, Zebco is in deep trouble."

Jim's frame stood in opposition to the frame or perspective in the organization at large:

"Because of our great success and the fame of our brand, Zebco will always continue to perform well in spite of the competition."

To make his frame persuasive, Jim had to use the following position:

"Asian competitors are changing the price and quality dynamics of the industry. They have the edge over us. As a result, Zebco will be forced to move its production from the United States to foreign lands."

The evidence Jim used consisted of a small number of tightly focused statistics benchmarking Zebco against its competition on production costs and quality measures.

To convince his employees about Zebco's dire future, Jim again took strong, symbolic actions. One morning at 7:15, soon after everyone arrived at the plant, all the lights in the factory suddenly went out. It was pitch dark, and then the national anthem began to play over the speaker system. A short while later, the lights returned, and Jim and his management team began to pass out American flags to everyone. On every flag was a small sticker that said "Made in Taiwan." Then they handed out red, white, and blue smocks to everyone with the words Zebco Quality Control Department printed on the back.

Jim came onto the factory floor and began to talk. The extinguished lights, he said, signified what could happen to Zebco: Due to foreign competition, it was a matter of time before the lights literally went out forever in this plant. Like the American flags they held in their hands, fishing tackle would all be made in a place like Taiwan. The company would be forced to move its production overseas, and the Zebco plants would close. American jobs would be lost forever. Jim went on to say that while the prices of Asian-made reels were going down, Zebco's prices were increasing every year.

You'll remember that I talked about using examples to support our arguments. What Jim did in this lights-and-flags action of his was to have the workforce experience vicariously a "live" example of the likely outcome of *not* taking action, of sticking with the organization's status-quo frame. By staging a plant closing as an actual event, he had his audience learn what it would feel like —a severe shock.

You'll remember that the main focus of any persuasion effort is to highlight *outcomes*—to tell our audience what to expect as the consequences of supporting our position and of not supporting it. This is where we have our greatest emotional impact. In this case, the "lights out" example was a horrendous outcome for the workers to contemplate, so it struck a powerful emotional chord. The small American flags suggested another dread outcome: that Asian competitors would take over Zebco's market. The Made in Taiwan tags made the point with brutal eloquence: If Americans no longer care that their flags are made by foreigners, will they feel any differently about their fishing gear?

Effective leaders, however, always offer optimistic outcomes as well for their positions. Continuing to speak to his audience, Jim explained that plant closings did not have to be the future of Zebco. The company had one last chance—to cut costs and raise quality. But these were things that only the employees could do.

"Afterward," said Betty Lang, a line worker who was there at the time Jim doused the lights and gave out flags, "there was a lot of talk about it. There was this sense of awe. Few of us had realized how serious the situation was. I had never thought about the lights going out. We just could not imagine such a thing happening. Then when the lights went out and with those Made in Taiwan American flags in our hands, we realized it could really happen.

"We could see the prices of reels from overseas compared to the prices of ours. They were cutting our throats. I think the event really convinced the doubters—that is, the majority of us. It really could happen—that's what we started to realize. And it could happen soon."

Jim then created another event—further evidence to dramatically support his frame. This one concerned the transfer of production to Mexico.

Before Jim's arrival, the company had opened a pilot production line in Mexico to take advantage of low labor costs there. The line had begun with the Zebco model 202, an inexpensive promotional reel that was easy to manufacture. The experiment had worked, and now the Brunswick Corporation, Zebco's parent company, was ready to move several more reels to Mexico. Long-range plans were in the works to eventually move even the Zebco model 33. That reel was the mainstay of the Tulsa operations. "The 33 has always been our bread-and-butter reel," Jim later explained. "That product essentially kept our plant going, because it was our best-seller." Moving that reel's production to Mexico would signify that the end was near for the Tulsa plant. It would simply become a distribution center for the company's products—nothing more. Hundreds of jobs would be lost.

Before the Mexican production line could begin assembly of the new reels, it needed several truckloads of parts and equipment. Jim ordered the trucks to be loaded at Zebco headquarters. Then he instructed the drivers to pull out of Tulsa and park their trailers at a truck stop some sixty miles away. He told them to sit tight until they heard from him.

He gathered the employees and told them that, as he spoke, more production was moving out to Mexico and that still more would soon follow—one day even the model 33, and thereafter the company's new models. All this was going to happen, he said, unless the employees could give the company a good reason for it not to happen.

"Jim told us that he didn't want to see this company go to Mexico," one employee remembered. "He said, 'I believe that we as an organization can keep this company here if we really want to. But it's going to take everyone in this plant to do it. I can't do it by myself, and you can't do it by yourselves. But if we work as a team, then we can make it happen.' "

The audience was stunned. The event crystallized the urgency of the situation. All along the workforce had imagined that Zebco would simply introduce new products to fill Tulsa's production gaps created by older models moving to Mexico. Jim was telling them otherwise. "I've got to make two phone calls," Jim told them. "One is to Brunswick. I want to be able to tell them that this workforce is ready to take responsibility for bringing down costs . . . to reinvent their whole way of doing things. I want to tell Brunswick I know we can do it. If that first call works, I'll make a second call, to bring back those trucks that are headed for the border."

The audience roared out its willingness, and when the trucks rolled back into headquarters, the workers greeted them with cheers. But it wasn't on the basis of just a crowd's reaction that Jim made his two calls. For months he had been meeting with the employees in small groups. He called them "six-on-one" meetings, because in each there had to be at least six employees to one Jim. That way they'd feel comfortable ganging up on him and being more candid. Each meeting lasted two hours. Jim began each of them the same way:

> I am the president of the company. I work for you,
> you are my board of directors. I'm now going to give you
> the financial status of your business here. You have

about $50 million invested, you get $200,000 a year in profit. However, the competition is coming on strong, and you're going to be losing money pretty soon unless you do something. Now if you sell the company—if you take that $50 million and convert it into cash, put it in the credit union—you can get at least $5 million—as compared with the $200,000 you're getting now. The $5 million is all you get!

So you've got a decision to make. You can keep Zebco going, or you can sell it.

At that point Jim paused and let the hard truth of those words sink in: Wouldn't any sane board of directors, faced with numbers like those, dump Zebco as fast as it could? Then he continued: "You directors have just hired me into this company and presented me with your dilemma. What should we do? Do we keep it or do we sell it?"

Jim then gave each person in the meeting five minutes to talk, after which there was an open discussion. The first reaction was almost always to sell, but then Jim got the group to figure out what the consequences of a sale would be: for them, no jobs.

In the second hour, Jim fielded questions from the group. He focused his answers on the actions that the company had to take to survive. "I didn't beat around the bush," he said later. "I said, 'Well, the fact is that you *are* losing your company. But there doesn't seem to be any sense of urgency among you to do anything about it. Yet the truth is, only you people can keep it from happening.'"

He walked each group through the entire cycle of Zebco's costs, from producing the reels to selling them. He explained why some reel production had already been sent to Mexico. He showed how Zebco's production costs were so much higher than production costs in foreign countries. He displayed newspaper ads that showed the actual sales prices of Zebco's reels versus the competition. Throughout, like Jan Carlzon of SAS, he used only a few key statistics to make his point.

The impact of these sessions was profound. "Before Jim arrived," one employee told me, "we'd have little talks with our managers, but management really didn't give us any solid reasons why we needed to be more responsive. But Jim was different. He really got right down to the grassroots and let every employee know what was happening. He showed us what was going on in the marketplace. He showed us how our production costs were affecting us in the marketplace, making us uncompetitive. . . . He told us that he did not want to see this company go to foreign countries.

"He said, 'I believe that we, as a company, can keep this company here, if we want to. But it's going to take everybody in this plant to do it.' He explained to us how we, as individuals on the shop floor, had a better opportunity to see where costs could be cut. We were in a better position to improve production because we *were* production. When you do a job every day, you know short-cuts, and you can find easier ways to do jobs that make it faster.

" 'It's up to you,' he told us, 'as well as me. I can't do it by myself, and you can't do it by yourselves. But if we work as a team, we can handle it.'

"Our reactions at the end of those meetings were strong. We told him flat out: You keep this company here and give us a chance."

Let's step back for a moment and look at what Jim is doing.

He knows that small groups will be a far more effective way to reach his workforce than large public forums. Small group size encourages candor and creates rapport. They let him build relationship and trust.

The tremendous time investment Jim is making in these small-group meetings shows his commitment—in actions. Employees sense he is really exerting himself to hear them out. Again, a terrific trust builder.

All this lays the groundwork for Jim's main persuasion effort: to get the workforce to believe in his approach to turning the company around.

Now let's look at his arguments in the individual meetings.

He puts his employees into the mindset of management. He gets them to be pragmatic about the company's narrowing options: to sell or to move. By drawing upon powerful evidence showing the growing advantages of Asian competitors, he induces them to come to grips with Zebco's declining future. What's important is that Jim's groups come to their conclusions through their own analysis, not because Jim commanded them.

By stressing that the employees must be the source of ideas to save the Tulsa operation, he reaffirms what they already believe to be true—that in many ways they know more about production than the company's managers. Once they accept that premise, however, they are led to an inevitable conclusion: Since they are the most knowledgeable, they must be the most responsible for implementing fundamental changes.

One other feature not easily captured by these descriptions of Jim's actions was that he gained great credibility through his emotional appeal. He spoke to the workers' deep pride in their country and their strong feelings about keeping jobs in America. This was shared ground: The workforce sensed Jim's own patriotism and his belief in the abilities of the American worker.

"Jim is a really good persuader," a worker said, "and you can trace it back to his sincerity. You can tell that he has a definite desire to see America stay the country it has always been and to keep people employed here.

"The other thing is that when Jim addresses a group you are fueled on his enthusiasm alone. You can't help but feel the electricity. He's saying that Zebco is more than a company that's building a product. We're building people, we're building an image, we're building reels in America, we're bringing back work to America that has been going the other direction. We want this product to be built in America, but also we want it to be purchased because it has value and quality that is better than the competition."

As a result of Jim's various actions, the Zebco workforce threw themselves into the task of saving the company. They began holding brainstorming sessions to find ways to cut production costs while pushing quality higher. Working with the company's engineers, teams of workers quickly uncovered ways to improve production machinery, to alter reel designs, and to change product materials. Soon production costs began to drop and quality to climb. By 1989, the turnaround had catapulted Jim to the presidency of Zebco.

Within fifteen years, Jim and his workers increased the size of Zebco sevenfold despite fierce Asian competition. Production efficiencies increased threefold and costs dropped. The Zebco 33 that sold for $29.95 in 1954 sells as low as $9.95 at stores today. In 1991 Zebco won the Wal-Mart vendor-of-the-year award distinguishing the firm as exceptional among Wal-Mart's 8,000 suppliers —the first sporting-goods company to be so honored and the first tackle company nominated in Wal-Mart's thirty-year history. In 1992, it won the award again. Altogether it was a remarkable set of achievements.

The Jim Dawson story has a message for each of us: Use actions to strengthen your persuasion. Use them, specifically:

1. to build your credibility more rapidly;
2. to craft events that magnify the emotional tone you want to convey;
3. to serve as examples of outcomes you're arguing will occur; and
4. to demonstrate your own commitment to your frames and positions.

You don't have to be a Jim Dawson to be an effective persuader. Brilliance always helps, of course, but persuasion is one human endeavor where careful attention to the basic principles pays off handsomely.

Once you switch from command to persuade, your whole style will change. You'll convince through a new understanding of the dynamics of dialogue and debate, and you'll convince by constructing positions that have wide appeal. You'll be talking less and listening more, alert for chances for practical compromise, knowing that compromise is often a pathway to support for your ideas.

It may seem hard at first, but it won't for long. As you use the techniques you've learned in this book, you'll absorb them and they'll become second nature for you. As they do, you'll find that your contacts with others, whether in business or in private life, will become less stressful and more productive. To a large extent good persuasion, with its emphasis on the needs and attitudes of the other person, is about mutual influence—individuals seeking the best outcomes for one another.

As organizations grow flatter and teams continue to become the work unit of the future, the skills of constructive persuasion will only grow in importance. Your ability to master this highly effective form of influence will translate into an investment that will pay handsomely into your future.

Appendix 1
The Passing
Age of
Command

A revolution is taking place, a historic shift in the nature of managing. Like it or not, you're caught in that revolution. It will greatly affect your life and livelihood. If you don't understand the revolution it may batter you. But if you do know what's in the process of happening, you'll have a better chance of surviving it and prospering.

The first two appendices will give you that vital context. In a few pages they tell you how the command system, which most people had always assumed was eternal, is being supplanted by a radically new approach and why. With this background you'll see that the persuasion techniques I have presented throughout this book aren't just superficial success ploys but fundamental principles of a transforming new mode of managing.

The Age of Command

The command age of management, once powerful and now in decline, had its roots in an institution called bureaucracy.

We tend to think of bureaucracy as one of those phenomena that have always existed, like motherhood and weather. The fact, however, is that bureaucracy—the fundamental structure of command management—had a known and specific beginning, many thousands of years ago in Sumer and Assyria in what is today the Near East. Kings and priests in those ancient societies were the first to build sophisticated administrative systems to control the multitudes. The militaries in those kingdoms were particularly skilled at perfecting bureaucracy. They waged war over vast territories of their known world, and the logistics for long-distance warfare were complex and demanding. They needed organizations that could command and supply large armies. Respect for directives from superiors was absolutely critical to the success of maneuvers involving thousands and thousands of soldiers.

From the start, military and civil leaders were closely linked. The early Roman republic required candidates for political office to have served ten years in the military or gone through ten military campaigns. Since nearly all civilian managers had had military experience and been raised in a society where a few individuals wielded enormous power, they saw managing by command as the natural way to run everything, including business.

Frederick the Great, who ruled Prussia from 1740 to 1786, contributed greatly to the rationale for command management. His armies were mixtures of all kinds of troublesome individuals— criminals, mercenaries, forced conscripts, and paupers. To shape these hodgepodges into disciplined organizations, he borrowed ideas from the Roman legions. He introduced ranks and uniforms; he standardized regulations and equipment; he instituted drills and devised a language of command. To guarantee that his soldiers would respond to commands instantly and unquestioningly, he insisted that they be "taught to fear their own officers more than the enemy."[1]

Frederick also created a distinction between command functions and advisory ones, exempting specialist advisers from the line of command so that they could freely and imaginatively plan activities—the prototype of staff functioning in today's corporations.[2]

His innovations spread to all of society and greatly influenced philosophies of leadership in business and a variety of other human endeavors. In 1832, Charles Babbage, an early inventor of the mathematical computer, published a paper arguing for a scientific approach to management. Just as Frederick had done, he suggested creating a division between labor and planning. Along with others later in the nineteenth century and in the early twentieth, he developed what today is called the classical, or scientific, management theory. He urged that labor be thought of not as people but as a machine that could be designed to maximize efficiency and output. Control centers, he said, must be established to direct this human machinery. Who held which job and who had the right to order others—these were choices that had to be carefully made to "ensure that when commands were issued from the top of the organization they would travel throughout the organization in a precisely determined way, to create a precisely determined effect."[3]

These ideas of the "modern management" thinkers, when combined with the military models upon which corporations were built, strengthened the institution of command management.

Nowhere was this mindset so pronounced as in the writings and theories of Frederick Taylor, an American management theorist of the late nineteenth century. A Harvard dropout, he joined the Midvale Steel Company in 1878 as a laborer apprentice and was quickly promoted to foreman. He became convinced that his coworkers rarely realized their potential work output and had little desire to. Taylor felt that a "scientific" system was needed if managers were to get the most out of their employees.[4]

He believed that companies were trapped in the mistaken notion that low wages meant lower production costs. He argued that, quite to the contrary, low wages were no guarantee of lower labor costs. Under his own scheme, labor costs would actually go down while wages went up. The key was to devise incentive plans that encouraged workers to work at their maximum speed. Taylor set up time-and-motion studies to analyze and standardize work activities, increasing efficiency by breaking jobs down into specialized duties. Laborers, in this view, were simply machine parts.

The impact of these ideas was eventually felt in enormous ways. The great assembly-line technologies pioneered by Henry Ford and others were shaped by scientific management. The mod-

ern-day, fast-food restaurant, where every step of hamburger manufacture and service is carefully timed and specialized, is another
example.

Taylor stressed the importance of hierarchical authority and
decision making in maximizing performance. One of scientific
management's central principles was to "shift all responsibility for
the organization of work from the worker to the manager." Taylor
was known to say to workers, "You are not supposed to think.
There are other people paid for thinking around here."

"Under our system," he wrote, "a worker is told just what he
is to do and how he is to do it. Any improvement he makes upon
the orders given to him is fatal to his success." He believed in
top-down commands—the notion that those above us know
what's best for us to do. Senior managers, he taught, should be
responsible for achieving results, while the lower ranks are meant
to meet the defined standards of performance. As in the military,
the private follows orders.

Many of this century's great entrepreneurs such as Henry
Ford and John D. Rockefeller, the men who shaped the modern
corporation, were classic command-style managers. Legions of
professional managers were schooled in their autocratic style of
leadership, with each level of managers simply passing commands
down the chain of authority.

The two world wars gave military training to several generations of executives. An example was the Ford Motor Company's
Whiz Kids—all former Army Air Force officers. Their experience
in uniform continued to encourage a managerial style based on
commands and respect for the hierarchy.

Nowhere was this more evident than at corporations like Procter & Gamble Company in the 1950s and 1960s. Its senior ranks
heavily populated with former military officers, Procter & Gamble
adopted an extreme form of command style. To get a project approved, a junior manager had to get approximately six signatures,
one from each of the managerial and executive levels above him.
At Ford, blue memo pads were reserved for executives, like epau-
lets on the shoulders of an officer's uniform. At IBM, water pitchers
in an office were like medals of honor awarded only to senior
managers. Each level's perks and authority were carefully defined,
just as in Frederick's armies and in the Roman legions.

I penetrated the mindset of this era through interviews with managers who started their careers in the 1950s and 60s. One was Mike Victor, an executive at a large New York bank who told me of his days as a young banker in the 1960s. His words portray the command era of just a generation ago:

> As a junior man I didn't even have an office, of course. I was out on what we then called a platform. Having an office was a sign of having really arrived. We wore white shirts only. We wore hats to and from the office; hats were considered part of the uniform. And of course we'd never dare take our suit coats off. Not even in our offices, if we had one. That was totally taboo.
>
> It was easy to manage in a strictly hierarchical setting like that, because that was the system that was in place then and that was the system that was honored, revered, feared, all of the above—both by those managing the hierarchy on top and by those who were on the rungs below. You always knew exactly where you stood. There was a built-in sort of incentive to go level by level by level. You'd go one at a time.
>
> There were sharp divisions of labor. Vice presidents and senior vice presidents discussed policy matters only among themselves. It was absolutely off-limits for them to talk about policy with junior people. The decisions of the senior people were never questioned by the juniors. You'd never say, "Does the president really know what he is doing with this particular thing?" That stuff was in the exclusive domain of the senior people.
>
> Relationships with bosses were much more formal than they are today. You'd work many, many years before referring to the vice president and certainly the senior vice president by their first names. There was always a very formal overtone to the whole thing, which, of course, was true with life in general in those days. Seniority almost always meant age as well as rank; your bosses were older than you were. I think the formality was necessary to support the hierarchical system.
>
> Sharing of secrets was much more restricted then.

Your discussions would be confined to the matter of the
day. If you happened to be working on a project for U.S.
Steel, your discussions with your seniors would usually
be limited quite narrowly to discussions about U.S. Steel.
Usually the senior's standard question at the end was,
"How are things going?" Well, today if a boss was to ask,
"How are things going?" and an employee wasn't very
happy or there was some issue of the day, he'd get an
earful. The junior would have no hesitation whatsoever
about launching right into it.

The world Mike Victor describes is the one that, until fairly
recently, shaped most managers. It was based on four assumptions:

1. Power and authority were vested in positions, not individuals; the more senior you became, the more of both you
   would possess, simply by virtue of your seniority.
2. Your rank ensured relatively unquestioned acceptance of
   your directives by the levels below you.
3. Directives and commands were the most effective and efficient means of leading others.
4. By obeying your seniors you paid your dues, entitling you
   to move up in due course and command the same respect.

In the turbulent 1960s and 1970s, however, when institutions
of all kinds were challenged as never before, these assumptions
were challenged, too. Competition became intense; companies had
to speed up their responsiveness to the marketplace. It was found
that the hierarchical/command style was too slow. It took too long
for decisions to move up and down the levels in the ordained
sequence. Working relationships became more informal. Employees developed minds of their own. They began to question more,
to assert themselves. They had less patience with the restrictions
of the hierarchical system and were less likely to defer to their
bosses automatically. A command boss could no longer manage
with the ease of just a decade prior.

To illustrate that change, Mike Victor compares the way a
restless, ambitious young bank employee would have been dealt

with a generation ago, when Mike was beginning his career, with the way he would be dealt with today:

In the old days the particularly assertive ones were pretty tame compared to how they are today. A restless junior employee would have gone to whomever he reported to and said, very politely, "Jack, I'm not sure I'm cut out for this," or whatever. Then Jack would have talked to *his* boss. That boss would have called the junior in and said, "Now, I understand from Jack that you're a little bit restless. Let's talk about it." The discussion would have been very circumspect. There were certain, unwritten codes of conduct about what the junior could and could not say. He could have said, "Well, I'd like to move along a little faster." That would have been perfectly acceptable.

The boss might have nodded sagely and said, "Well, your day will come if you work hard." He'd have given the junior a be-patient lecture mentioning all the good things that would come with time. Or he could have said, "Well, now, Dave, you don't think you're moving along fast enough. Let me say that *we* think you're doing very well, and may I remind you of your high performance ratings and how highly the bank thinks of you?" It was always sort of third person—the reference to how the bank thinks about you and how your seniors have a very high regard for you and all of that.

In other words, you'd have been held at arm's length, and there wouldn't have been much you could do about it. The boss held all the cards. The junior might have meekly said, "Well, if it wouldn't be out of line, sir, I wonder if I could have a little more direct responsibility with clients." And that might or might not have ended up being factored into some short-term plan for you.

Today's generation, however, comes on very differently and with an entirely different set of expectations. This afternoon I have a meeting with a young man who is stewing over whether he should stay at the bank. He's a very bright, impatient fellow who doesn't think he's moving as fast as he should. He's going to tell me, in no uncertain terms and in a lot of detail, why he doesn't think he has enough responsibility. And why he thinks that he may go to Goldman Sachs because he's heard that in 1.8 years you can be at a certain position there, and you can be making this amount of money and so on.

Thirty years ago a boss just wouldn't have been exposed to that sort of challenge from a junior.

With great speed, this new attitude about appropriate relationships with one's superiors is undermining the command model of managing.[5] In today's business environment, in fact, a command style actually has the potential to backfire. Take the case of Sunbeam-Oster.[6]

In 1990 the Sunbeam-Oster company, then called Allegheny, lost $40 million. Through a buyout, Paul B. Kazarian came in from an outside investment partnership to become CEO. He did a remarkable job of selling off money-losing divisions and focusing the company's attention on its appliance operations. By the very next year he had turned the $40 million loss into a $47 million profit.

By late 1992, with its third-quarter profits up 40 percent—to $12 million on sales of $200 million—the firm seemed headed for another incredible year. Analysts were glowingly predicting that Sunbeam's sales would grow by an additional 8 percent in 1993 to over $1 billion and that profits would climb 40 percent to $86 million.

For his success in streamlining the once debt-burdened firm, the board decided that in January 1993 they'd give Kazarian a $1 million bonus on top of his annual $1.75 million salary. But in January Mr. Kazarian got something quite different—the ax.

He wasn't the only one. At the time a wave of CEO firings and resignations was rolling through big business. Prominent executives such as Ken Olsen of Digital, Robert C. Stempel of General Motors, James D. Robinson of American Express, Joseph "Rod" Canion of Compaq Computer, and Paul Lego at Westinghouse were all out. At first glance Kazarian seemed just another instance.

But there was one remarkable difference. The other CEOs all shared problems that Kazarian didn't have—big financial or market-share losses and a failure to change the company as their boards wished them to. Most of their companies were bleeding red ink and in organizational crisis. Sunbeam, unlike any of the others, was a turnaround success.

Kazarian's problem was not corporate performance but his management style. Among his managers, stories abounded about his misdeeds. When he picked up a pint of orange juice and threw it at a manager, the word swept through the offices. So did reports of how he pitted executives against one another and tried to humiliate them with crass language. One day he took a BB gun—a product sample under consideration—and fired it at the empty chairs of company executives in the boardroom; with each shot he shouted, "Die!"

Finally his managers rebelled. *The Wall Street Journal* described what happened next:

> Six of Mr. Kazarian's top lieutenants, having pledged themselves to a "blood pact," initiated talks with the board after they and other managers endured a lengthy Saturday session with Mr. Kazarian on December 19 in which he is said to have berated them, called one of them "scum" and tried to enlist them in a campaign to undermine James Clegg, president of the company's largest division, household products. Getting together later, the managers agreed that "if one of us gets shot, we all get shot," as the conspirators put it. "We tell the board about what's been going on and then they'll decide: Either they get rid of him or we all leave." Other executives soon joined the blood pact. As board members listened to their report, they quickly realized that Paul Kazarian had to go. And he did. They fired him.

The Kazarian case is not unique. If you glance through the business pages you will find more and more stories like it. In my role as a consultant, I often see examples of backlash against command-style bosses, though few as sensational as the one at Sunbeam-Oster. Twenty years ago, when the command style was still universally accepted, Kazarian's successful record would have protected him. But today we are witnessing a dramatically lower tolerance for the Marine boot camp approach to managing. Your position in the hierarchy and your record of successes are no longer enough to guarantee you the respect and obedience of subordinates. What was a birthright for previous generations of managers is now just a memory.

Recently the forty-four-year-old vice president of human resources at a large manufacturing corporation made a comment to me that said it all. "You wouldn't believe how much harder my job has become," he said. "I used to think that by the time I reached this level all I had to do was to give directives and things would happen. That approach just doesn't work any longer. The biggest challenges are the young people. They're always asking me 'Why?' They're like my four-year-old son. When I started out, everybody believed in the boss's authority. No longer."

Many managers I meet are having experiences like these with their employees, and these same frustrations. Many feel as if their formal authority is evaporating. Gone are their days of being The Boss. Younger managers seem more self-directed and harder to motivate. Getting a commitment from them takes far more convincing. Though they are technically subordinates, they think nothing of going directly to their boss's boss or to his peers if they have a question or complaint.

"The day when you could yell and scream and beat people into good performance," said Allied Signal CEO Lawrence Bossidy, "is over. Today you have to appeal to them by helping them see how they can get from here to there, by establishing some credibility, and by giving them some reason and some help to get there. Do all those things, and they'll knock down doors."[7]

What happened to Paul Kazarian is just one of the unpleasant things that can happen to those who often rely on commands. Here are some others:

1. The command manager will find himself overloaded with decisions to make. Command management encourages upward delegation of decisions by staff. Ever fearful of the

consequences of a mistake, subordinates typically defer to the command manager. Decisions that could have been made on lower levels flow to the top.

2. The command manager makes his staff people less effective by starving them of information they need to make good decisions. That's because he's usually an information hoarder. He needs to feel "in control" and views information as a means to control and power. As a result, he is reluctant to share necessary data. In an age demanding decentralized and responsive decision making, this behavior can mean big trouble for both the manager and his organization.

3. The command manager will hear only the "good news," the news he wishes to hear. Other information will generally be sealed off from him because subordinates won't want to risk displeasing him. In an age where speed and quality of information are crucial, this is a recipe for disaster.

4. The command manager's most talented staff will gradually leave him, and he will find it increasingly difficult to attract new talent. Instead, at a time when teams are the favored approach, the best people will be drawn to the growing number of team-oriented managers. For the command manager, that will be a serious problem; as does every manager, he will rise or fall according to his ability to find talented people to work with.

5. In the command manager's group, creativity will be stifled. Subordinates will interpret his commands as placing restrictions on what they can explore and propose and as silencing perspectives that are out of the ordinary. Yet today competitive advantage often involves non-traditional and creative approaches. By dampening creativity, a manager jeopardizes not only the organization's long-term success but also his own career.

6. The command manager's staff will find ways to undermine him publicly and privately. Like Kazarian's colleagues, today's workers are far more willing to challenge—though not always directly—the command manager. With employee loyalty hitting all-time lows, staff willingness to get

back at a bad boss has increased significantly. Negative private interactions with employees will increasingly become
public affairs.

These various outcomes will have a cumulative impact. Command managers will find themselves reaching a plateau in their
careers or being forced out of their organizations. The process will
take place at an ever-increasing pace, because of a certain trait that
command managers share: They try to tighten their control in
times of change, and these are indeed times of change. Their efforts
only multiply their difficulties; the very actions they take to solve
their problems make them worse.

This is not to say that commands will never work. They will,
in special circumstances:

1. Situations where you are the only expert. But even here
   your talented people will stay with you only long enough
   to learn from you. And in an era where expertise must be
   constantly updated and seldom rests in a single individual,
   this will be an increasingly rare situation.
2. Environments where few other job opportunities exist for
   your staff, either inside or outside your company. Morale,
   however, will always suffer under a steady diet of commands.
3. Brief crisis situations that require immediate attention and
   control.
4. Jobs built around immediate demands, such as newsrooms
   or hospital emergency rooms, where commands based on
   expertise are acceptable.

Increasingly, the first two contexts are growing rarer. There
are more and more experts with whom one can work. And there
is plenty of competition to take away our most talented staff. Even
brief crisis situations now more often tend to become longer-term
ones. Though most of us have a short-term tolerance for commands during a period of crisis, that acceptance tends to wear thin
quickly.

In sum, command managers are an endangered species in

North America. Their habitat is steadily shrinking. The forces that are overturning the Age of Command and creating a new environment are so pervasive and so self-reinforcing that it will be difficult to turn back the clock.

Appendix 2
The New Age
of Persuasion

Peter Drucker was recently asked by the *Harvard Business Review* what managers need to know to manage well in this new and more challenging world. "You have to learn to manage in situations where you don't have command authority," he said, "where you are neither controlled nor controlling. That is the fundamental change."[1]

That's a good summary of the revolution I have just been describing. The new system Drucker describes is radically different from the system that reigned so long and until recently went unquestioned. A thoughtful person would have to wonder what kind of factors could have revolutionized managing so drastically and so fast.

The first and most important factor, as we've noted, is the impact of greater competitiveness in all areas of business. A "command and control" organization, with its upward delegation of decisions and its bureaucracy, slows reaction time and grows costs without adding value. It is a dinosaur in an age of nimble-footed, lean competitors. Extinction is not far off.

The second force is the new set of generational expectations.

Quite simply, Baby Boomers and Generation Xers are suspicious of hierarchy. They prefer more informal arrangements. They prefer to judge on merit rather than on status.

The third is the explosion in information technology. It allows junior managers access to the very top of an organization—by-passing bosses and the chain of command.

Workplace teams are of course the final force. While speeding the response to the competition, they are also bringing together managers who are no longer the formal bosses of one another.

All these forces are creating the future organization—*an organization of peers.* Not bosses, not subordinates, but peers. In this new organization, we manage not by the power of our position but by the power of our ideas and our persuasion.

Since much has been written about the first of these forces, the new competitive environment, we'll turn to the three less-talked-about forces: changes in workplace generations, the electronic erosion of authority, and the rise of the cross-functional team. In the process of this exploration we'll see why persuasion is swiftly supplanting the command approach.

Force Number One: Changes in the Workplace Generations

Each generation living today went through a set of experiences unique to itself. The Silent Generation, for example, composed of those born between 1925 and 1942, were the children of families that went through the Great Depression; they were influenced by their parents' hardships to treasure employment and be obedient employees, and by their parents' military service in World War II to be command-oriented.[2]

Following the Silent Generation came the well-publicized Baby Boomers, the group born between 1943 and 1960. Raised on rock and rebellion in an era of phenomenal national wealth, they became an indulged and somewhat narcissistic tribe and were nicknamed in adulthood Yuppies.

The most recent generation, born between 1961 and 1981, is called Generation X, or sometimes the Busters, because of the drop-off or "bust" in baby births following the Boomer generation. They are the children of dual-career parents and of parents whose marriages produced record national divorce rates. In contrast to the Boomers, who in college tended to major in liberal arts, this group chose majors in business and economics. In short, they spurned the idealism their parents had embraced when young for a more pragmatic and cynical realism.

These last two generations are now moving into important management roles. Boomers are becoming the senior executives of corporations, while Generation Xers are becoming their frontline managers. The impact on the command management system is enormous.

The Baby Boomers

At age forty, Michael Johnson is the youngest CEO to head the Canadian subsidiary of one of the world's largest pharmaceutical companies. He is also at the forefront of a wave of Baby Boomer bosses now filling the executive suites of North American corporations. A former hockey player, Michael stands tall and is physically imposing. Perfectly groomed, he looks the part of a young CEO. As he speaks, you hear the confidence in his voice, yet there is also a reflectiveness that hints at a different breed of company president.

In many ways, Michael is the epitome of the Baby Boomer executive. Deeply concerned about teamwork and participation, he believes in the egalitarian organization:

> I grew up with autocratic leadership—top-down management. I found in those situations that there are always winners and losers and that it doesn't necessarily resolve issues effectively or move an organization forward. For me, there's a lot wrapped up in the word "boss." People of my generation are negative on the word. We don't want to be a "boss."
>
> When people ask me what I do, I say I'm with so and so company. I don't say I'm the president. You don't take pride in being a boss over people. What you take

pride in is the accomplishments of your organization and how you help people's daily lives.

So my style is to be very involved with other people. I prefer to get expert opinions before having to impose a decision. I'm not afraid to impose one if I have to, but I like to involve others in the decision process. You'll get a better solution that way.

Within the space of a single generation, then, words like "boss" and "president" have completely changed their meanings. No longer positive signs of accomplishment and authority, they now symbolize distance from others, an unreasonable toughness, and other unattractive attributes.

Compared to executives of previous generations, Michael and his cohorts are distinctly different in style and attitude, and it shows in small ways as well as large ones. After a luncheon interview with Michael, I watched him climb into the front seat of his chauffeured company car so that he could be "up front" with the driver he knew. The next week I had lunch with a sixty-year-old president of a retailing company. This executive, though his driver had been with him for years, slipped into the back seat of his chauffeured company car. In the simple choice of where they sat, both men had made subtle statements about how they regarded their employees down the line. Those differing statements revealed the profound shift that has occurred during the space of a single generation.

What we are experiencing is a remarkable historical event, a pivotal change between the generations in their attitude toward authority. It began with the Baby Boomers and continues today with the Busters, setting these two generations distinctly apart from innumerable generations that went before.

The Boomers' parents were mostly members of The Silent Generation. A majority of the Silents were raised by people who had served in the military and had great respect for it, people who had seen strong and admired political and military leaders win a world war and restore the well-being of the society. Brought up in homes with those values and heroes, the Silents were predisposed to respect formal authority. They readily accepted the command model. So loyal were they to the corporation, in fact, that they came to be called "organization men."

But all of that changed with their children, the Baby Boomers. The Boomers had an entirely different experience of the world; they saw the vulnerability of authority. Instead of a victorious triumph over Nazi Germany, they witnessed a failed war in Vietnam, a series of assassinations, a disgraced president, an economic breakdown following the OPEC oil crisis, and environmental disasters like Three Mile Island. For this generation, authority looked increasingly unreliable and often just plain wrong.

They soon made their disenchantment apparent. In their music and manners they displayed contempt for leadership. They took to the streets and invaded college administration offices to protest. This kind of challenge to authority would have been unimaginable to their Silent Generation parents.

The Boomers' reluctance to accept formal authority tracks back to a trait implanted during their childhoods. Throughout the whole century in the United States, independence had become more and more desirable to parents as a character attribute for their children. In 1890 only 16 percent of parents believed that independence was an important quality; by the end of the 1970s, however, approximately 75 percent of all parents felt that independence was *the most important* character trait. As independence grew in importance, its antithesis—obedience—diminished steadily as a valued character trait.[3]

What forces were creating this stress on independence? One was the vulnerability of authority in society, as just described. A second was the growing affluence of North American society. People had more money for the services and machinery needed to run a household. That made them less dependent on family and community. Fathers were transferred by their companies across the nation, and this mobility further encouraged self-sufficiency.

Dr. Spock's Baby and Child Care, a book published in 1946, put strong emphasis on teaching children to be independent. Over the next decade it became massively influential. In the 1960s came the commercial introduction of the contraceptive pill, which gave women a greater sense of control and aided the emergence of the women's movement. For many women, these events spelled autonomy.

Education, too, undercut traditional authority. The Baby Boomers were beneficiaries of the greatest surge in education in history. Since 1960, the percentages of men and women graduating from high school have doubled and, from college, considerably more than doubled.[4] The new hordes in college and graduate school found themselves encouraged to critique the books and ideas they were studying. They were actually graded on their ability to challenge one another's thinking, and often the professor's.

These changes created a new breed of business person. The editor of *Fortune*, Walter Kiechel III, caught it perfectly. "As managers," he wrote, "and with remarkable consistency across the group, they espouse values that any progressive organization would endorse: lots of communication, sharing of responsibility, respect for others' autonomy. . . . They are also thoroughly uncomfortable with much of what has traditionally . . . been thought of as the leader's role. They don't like telling others what to do any more than they like being told. As bosses, they can be just as controlling as prior generations . . . but they're sneakier about it. [They are] no respecters of hierarchy."[5]

Generation X

Marie is fresh from college and now training to become a corporate banker. Well educated, a child of divorced parents, she embodies many of the characteristics associated with her generation. She likes to work hard and to do well—but to a point.

> I'm definitely willing to work long hours during the week, but there's a limit. You need some time for yourself, for your family, for recreation. With people my age there's more concern about quality of life. It's not really wanting the big, expensive vacation, it's just wanting to enjoy life. It's not just a matter of having more things. It's related to the uncertainty of life. Life is just not the way it was in the fifties and sixties. There are so many nasty things that can happen along the way. There's disease, there's crime—I mean, you're bombarded so constantly with all these negative aspects, it makes you think you might as well enjoy some of life.

This set of values may change as Generation Xer's move into midlife, when career demands soar, but for the present it appears to be a trademark of Xers. Interview after interview with this generation confirms a willingness to work hard but not always at the expense of one's personal life.

The attitude is rooted in the childhood homes of Xers and in the organizations where their parents work. For one thing, they tend to be children of parents both of whom held jobs. The Xers benefited from the extra family income these dual careers produced, but they felt deprived of their parents' company, a situation aggravated by the fact that a very high percentage of them were children of divorce. This was mainly because more of their mothers earned income of their own and had fewer of the worries about the poverty that can come with divorce.

Generation X appears not to want the sort of lives their parents led. They want to build more traditional families and be more available to their children. As a twenty-five-year-old manager explained to me: "You really need to be careful not to give a hundred percent of yourself to the job, or else there will be nothing left over for your partner when you get home at the end of the day." Having time at home with the family is a priority they felt their parents set too low. Consistently in interviews, I heard the comment: "We are not living to work but working to live. We are choosing a life as opposed to just bringing home a paycheck."

This attitude makes Generation X far less willing to identify closely with any organization. They like to think of themselves as an independent lot who can move if they don't like where they are.

In the Age of Command, you made sacrifices in your personal life to demonstrate your loyalty to the company. The rewards were often promotions and the power to command others. This kind of contract means little to Generation X. If you're not into command, why make extreme sacrifices?

The second set of forces undermining Generation X's regard for formal authority was unleashed by the corporations themselves. Just as the Xers were graduating from college, the wave of corporate downsizing began, with companies unceremoniously dumping longtime employees on the sidewalk. The Xers rightly sensed that company loyalty was definitely a thing of the past. The contract of lifetime employment that began to deteriorate for the Boomers feels practically nonexistent for the Xers.

They make their attitude very clear when you ask them about their career expectations. Generation Xers will tell you they expect to have—easily—three to five employers over their career. Ask them why so many and they'll say they expect, at some point, to lose their jobs. The corporate downsizing that tumbled their parents has made painfully evident to them how easily one can lose a job.

Talk with them further and you'll encounter their belief that you get better opportunities, better salaries, better challenges, and better locations not by waiting patiently to move up the ladder but by moving to another company. As did their Boomer parents, they believe that your loyalty is to yourself and your teammates, not to the boss or the company.

For this new generation, work is more than ever before a transaction. Their parents saw working hard and "following orders" as an investment likely to yield greater responsibility and rewards. Generation X expects a more immediate payout from their employer. The words of a senior banker sum it all up:

> The people who are my age [basically Boomers] have been with the bank for a while. There is an understanding that we are very committed to this organization and that we all truly want to work together to make this company work. Over and over again I've seen people put the organization ahead of their personal objectives. But with the analysts, the associates, the junior officers [Generation X], the commitment to this organization is not necessarily there. Instead you have to continually show them what it is they're getting out of this organization. Continually you have to *make it a two-way street.* That's the way you get their commitment. Commanding this generation won't do much to motivate them. They've got to be informed and convinced and involved. If you want their commitment, you've got to persuade them.

Force Number Two:
The Electronic Erosion of Authority

Another very important factor determining Boomer and Generation X management styles is sitting on your desk looking straight at you: the personal computer.

An employee's computer lets him "network" throughout all levels of an organization and to access up-to-date information from almost anywhere. E-mail and the various groupware programs such as Lotus Notes have sped the process. Some 22 million office PCs had been networked by the end of 1995, an increase of 54 percent from 1992.

While the obvious competitive advantage of information technology is *speed* of response, the advantage to managers within an organization will be *access*. As the futurist Alvin Toffler notes, it is now possible for a junior employee at the bottom of an organization to communicate directly with senior-level executives working on the same problem. Individuals can send requests for information of all sorts anywhere in a firm and receive requests themselves. Top executives can push a button or two on their computers and find themselves in touch with any member of their organization, to examine a spreadsheet or write a proposal together, discuss the week's sales results, or explore ideas for a new product.[6]

What all of this technology does is to distribute information in a radically new way. Information becomes more open and its delivery free of hierarchical norms. As that happens, relationships inevitably become less hierarchical.

Take, for example, the impact of network software at the insurance company Johnson & Higgins. Mary Jo Dirkes, a young staff member, posted a thoughtful message about the company's special efforts on workers' compensation. It brought her recognition and praise from the company's senior executives, and her responsibilities were broadened. Prior to networking at the company, says senior vice president John Deitchman, "I wouldn't have thought of going to her for help because she's relatively new and hadn't developed the traditional network of personal contacts in the firm."[7] Information technology gave Mary Jo instant access to senior levels that would not have been possible even ten years ago. She did not have to earn her stripes by a time-consuming climb up the hierarchy; she got them through the effectiveness of her suggestions and her access to the company network.

Hand in hand with greater access to information, however, goes the erosion of the power and authority of executives who once controlled that data. When people begin losing power they usually fight back. But with information technology, fighting back is likely in the long run to undermine an executive's credibility and ultimately his or her organization's competitiveness.

One young manager I studied, named Chris, worked for a billion-dollar company that distributes electronic parts. He monitored the creditworthiness of customers and the overall inventory to see what was selling and what wasn't. He'd then forecast sales to make sure the levels of inventory were appropriate. Along with twelve other asset managers, he reported directly to an operations vice president. Between Chris and his vice president, there were two key differences: One was age—Chris was thirty and his boss was fifty-two—and the other was computer literacy. Chris was literate, and the boss was not.

Once a month, the vice president handed Chris a thousand-page computer printout to review. It took Chris four to five days to examine manually as he searched for problems such as ballooning inventories of a certain part, or credit difficulties. One day, Chris asked the vice president for a copy of the computer diskette that had produced the thousand-page printout. With the diskette, he knew, he could do his job a lot quicker. The vice president was reluctant, but after Chris pressed for several days, the vice president handed it over.

Chris then performed in three hours what had previously taken him five days. Not only that. As he went along searching the database for credit problems, he took the opportunity to perform other analyses. He discovered some disturbing surprises, ones the vice president was ignorant of. He learned, for example, that certain electronic parts were being purchased for which there were either diminishing orders or none at all. In some cases, these errors were costing the company tens of thousands of dollars per part.

Chris brought his discoveries to the vice president. The vice president seemed uncomfortable, and the following month he denied him access to the diskettes. Shocked by this response, Chris saw the implications of his simple request:

> The vice president realized that it gave him information that he was totally unaware of. It would have taken him six weeks to do manually what I did in two hours. What he also realized is that I could replace him—because I knew what questions to ask of the computer. Imagine what I could do if I had total access. He wouldn't be needed anymore.
>
> But this vice president is about to become the fall guy. The president is now saying, "I can't understand what the problem is in operations. You keep hiring these high-priced asset managers, but the same problems have kept reappearing over the last two years. I'm going to hire a new director of asset managers, somebody who can get to the heart of this."
>
> But the secret is out. The other VPs had access to my report. They've seen what the computer can do, and they know my results didn't take eight weeks to produce. They're coming to me asking how to get the same information. One of these days it's going to be revealed that the vice president is the one holding all the horsepower back. But by that time, it will be too late. A third of our asset managers have already left, and I figure the rest of us will be gone soon. Another asset manager and myself are leaving in a week.

Journalist Thomas Stewart captured the dilemma: "Just about as big a mistake [as failing to exploit information technology] is trying to play the new game by the old command-and-control rules. Networks are characterized by openness, and the genie won't go back into the bottle. The only way to keep control over information is to make the network hard to use—for example, by restricting who can send mail to whom—thereby defeating its purpose."[8]

Information technology means that your subordinates will

increasingly have access to the same information you do. They will have the potential to do more of your job than ever before and in a more sophisticated manner. In essence, they will be "better educated." They will also see more clearly how well you are performing.

These new perspectives will encourage them to assess your ideas and insights more critically, further stripping away the old automatic and unconscious respect for the position of the boss, which you may have been relying on. They will be less likely to accept an order without first asking why. You'll have to be far more thoughtful and persuasive in how you argue for your solutions and ideas.

Force Number Three: The Team-Based Organization

The team-based organization is the management system of the future, the business world's response to the need for speed in an ever more competitive environment. Japanese automobile manufacturers can go from design to production in less than 60 percent of the time that most car manufacturers require. In part, this is due to the involvement of cross-functional expertise early on in the design process. One American jet engine manufacturer I studied cut the time it needed to engineer and produce a new engine model in half simply by introducing cross-functional teams to the process. Cross-functional teams are speed machines.

Before teams came along, ingredients were added to new products step by step. The R & D department tinkered with an initial idea. The result of that tinkering was handed off to the engineering department. While engineering might have liked some of R & D's ideas, they often found them a bit unworkable for the actual product. So they made major changes. After the engineers designed their "workable" product, the marketing people typically took one look at it and declared they had no markets for such a thing. However, they said, if the engineers would go back to their drawing boards and reconfigure the design with the following features, then perhaps some customers could be found. At later phases, other areas also had their say—sales, finance, manufacturing, and so on—each of them wanting changes.

In an era when the competition moved at a snail's breath, this slower pace worked, despite its wastefulness. But as new competitors from Asia and Europe appeared on the horizon, the rules began to change. Getting to market faster with fresher, better-designed products soon became a competitive necessity. And the cross-functional team was born.

When you watch effective cross-functional teams, you quickly realize the source of their speed. In a single setting, they maximize the number of perspectives on a given issue. They are in essence information-generating devices. From this multifunctional pool of information, better initiatives flow quite naturally and in compressed time.

As we've seen with Jack and Kevin in our opening chapter, the team approach is the ultimate challenge to the old traditions of power and authority. The people seated across from us at the meeting table are likely to be our functional peers from marketing, finance, production, and so on. In most cases, there will be an appointed leader, but he will probably have the title rather than the power. After all, the leader is a peer, not a boss.

How do you lead peers? It sounds like a contradiction in terms. Yet it can be done. You do it with a different kind of leadership.

You won't be ordering people to do things; you don't have the authority. But you can influence them with up-to-date expertise or by bringing needed resources to the discussion. You can do it by building strong personal relationships with the people around the table. You can do it by becoming a master persuader.

Appendix 3
LET'S GET IN THERE AND FIGHT!

We have to fight in a stagnating market.

We have to fight competitors who are more efficient than we are.

And who are at least as good as we are in figuring out the best deals.

We can do it. But only if we are prepared to fight. Side by side.

We are all in this together.

Jan Carlzon

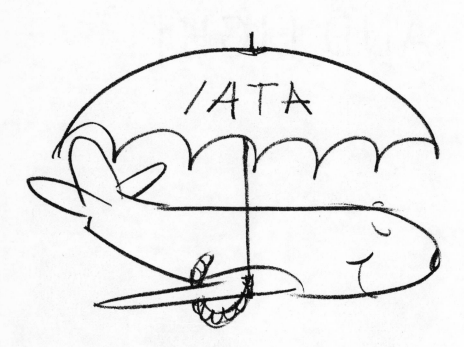

We were a healthy, profitable company for 17 years.

Business boomed, year after year.

In IATA, we and the other airlines pretty much agreed on how we would share the increasingly abundant bag of goodies.

It was a secure and orderly world.

Who was to know there were storm clouds beyond the horizon?

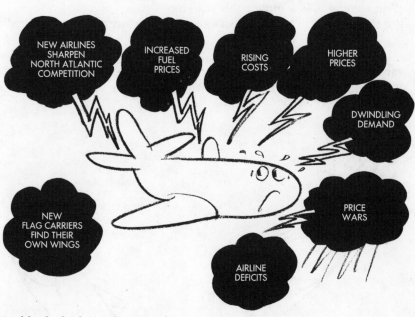

Suddenly, bad weather struck . . .

The airline lost $12 million last year.
   We are going to lose money this year, too.
   But then it's got to stop. We can't afford to lose any more!

We are in bad shape. But we haven't reached the crisis point yet.
   If we were, we wouldn't know how to get our nose up again.

But we can. If we are ready to fight for our jobs and our future, we can recover.

It won't be easy.

 We are bearing a lot of unnecessary costs originating from our comfortable days under IATA's protection. Now we have to trim the fat.

We've got some tough competition. Like the "street fighters" from the rough-and-tumble American domestic market. Efficient. In shape. Like Delta . . .

Or European companies which have pursued more consistent and purposeful policies than we have. And who keep making money, hard times
or not.

Look at the differences:

Key figures *	Swissair INTERNATIONAL	SAS INTERNATIONAL
Cabin Factor	63.6	59.3
Load Factor	59.2	57.8
Passenger revenue (USD)/RPK	0.09	0.08
Cargo revenue (USD)/RFTK	0.37	0.31
Total revenue (USD)RTK	0.79	0.73
Operating cost (USD)/ATK	0.45	0.42
Revenue-Cost Relationship (Over 100—pront)	103.5	99.7
Average flight leg/km	1051	967

* USD—U.S. Dollars. RPK—Revenue Passenger-kilometers, RFTK—Revenue Freight Tonne-kilometers. RTK—Revenue Tonne-kilometers. ATK—Available Tonne-kilometers.
Exchange rate: one USD—4.65 Swedish kronor.

Delta has:

○ 40% more revenue tonne-kms per employee

○ 120% more passengers per employee

○ 14% more available tonne-kms per pilot

○ 40% more passenger-kms per cabin attendant

○ 35% more passenger-kms per passenger sales employee

It is difficult to make similar comparisons in the technical and maintenance fields, but even in these areas Delta has a substantially higher productivity than SAS.

This is what we have to do:

Right now, we look like this:

Income	$1,505 million
Expenses	$1,517 million
Deficit	$12 million

Next year, we should look at least this good:

Income	$1,517 million
Expenses	$1,505 million
Profit	$12 million

And in just a few years, that profit should be $120 million, at least!

We'll be in bad shape if we don't make it.

This is how we are going to do it!

We have to consolidate.

We have to be market-oriented.

We have to be more efficient.

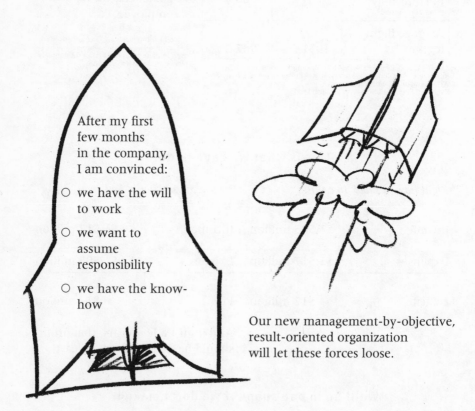

After my first
few months
in the company,
I am convinced:

○ we have the will
to work

○ we want to
assume
responsibility

○ we have the know-
how

Our new management-by-objective,
result-oriented organization
will let these forces loose.

The new organization won't solve any problems in itself.
It is merely a prerequisite if we are to work more efficiently.

The organization will open the vents and let responsibility and authority take off all over the company.
And liberate initiative and determination. So we can all take off.

No more friction!

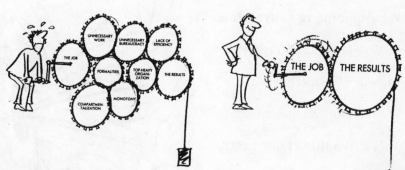

The new organization is designed to get results.
This requires efficiency.
To eliminate friction. We have to pitch in and do away with the kind of work we no longer need.
The kind that diverts our energy, time and money from important business.
The repair job is starting now, and the wheels will be ready to roll in September.

We are going to be much more punctual. Everyone can help.

"Operation Punctuality" is starting soon. It's going to give everyone a chance to help make us one of Europe's most punctual airlines.

We are going to consolidate.

O With fewer aircraft types

O With a "cleaner" network

O With more profitable routes

This will help cut our costs.

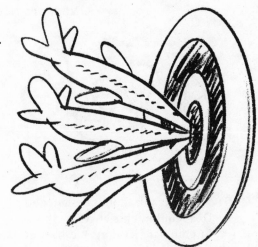

We are going to zero in on the business travel market.

○ It's big.

○ It's demanding.

○ It's where the money is.

Above all, we are going to capture the business travel market in Scandinavia—our home market. Half of it today is in the hands of our competitors.

This is what we're going to do for Business Class:

Ticket Offices
Special phone numbers.
High-level service at ticket counters.

Check-in
Simplified check-in for passengers
with carry-on baggage only.
Separate check-in counters for
Business Class.
Seat selection.
High service level, shorter lines.
Quicker check-in procedures.
Special baggage tags.

Service Lounge at Kastrup
Telephone, telex services (debited).
Ticketing (Help with rebookings).
Office space.
Coffee shop.
SAS News Bulletin Board.
Wardrobe for winter clothes.
Message Service.

Embarkation
Economy Class passengers board first
Business Class passengers board last.
Gate manager to assist passengers.

Debarkation
Business Class first.

Business Class Service on Board

Separate cabin.
Improved seating comfort.
Enclosed hat racks.
Improved meal service.
Free beverage service.
More personal service from cabin attendants (freed from collecting for drinks).
New, more informative in-flight announcements.
Improved newspaper service.
Tax-free sales always starting in Business Class.

Better Punctuality

Cut the Mad Dash at Kastrup

Shuttle Services to and from Kastrup

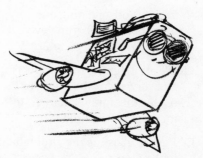

Increased cargo revenue will beef up the bottom line. Cargo marketing will be more efficient as a result-oriented sector *all its own*.

We are going to raise our pleasure-travel revenues as well.

We've got some attractive proposals up our sleeves for the holiday market.

We are also out for better marginal business, like more profitable charters . . .

When you put it all together . . .   **. . . that should do it.**

○ We are slashing unnecessary costs.

○ We are improving our efficiency.

○ We are consolidating our operations and cutting even more costs.

+2%

○ We are tailoring our products and service for the needs of the big business travel market, to increase our income.

A 2% improvement means some $30 million. With that much in our pockets, we've taken the first step toward a new, profitable SAS.

○ We are boosting our profitability with cargo and tourism.

○ We are grabbing every opportunity for marginal business.

○ We are going to find it's more fun to work.

We've got to help each other:

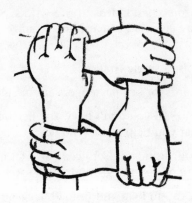

If anything goes wrong, the customer doesn't care whose fault it is. He's the one who's going to suffer anyway.

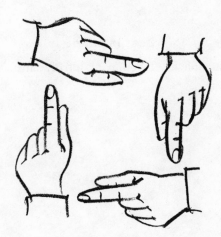

If we help each other, we can put just about anything right and spare our customers a lot of grief.

But we've got to work together!

Don't wait. Start Now!

We've got a lot of projects and ideas in the works. Some will start right away, and others may take half a year to materialize. Don't wait. Make it happen, now!

○ Sell SAS. Don't miss a single chance.

○ Bend over backwards for our passengers at our stations.

○ Help your colleagues. If you don't have any personal contact with our customers, see that you help those who do.

○ On board, give your utmost in service. Don't let off a single unhappy passenger: Your friends on the ground will back you up!

○ Do whatever you can to load and unload baggage on time, so we can maintain our timetables.

○ Plan maintenance and overhaul so our aircraft will be ready to go on schedule.

○ Start today!

Bear in mind:

The only really valuable asset we have is a truly satisfied customer.

Notes

Chapter 1.

1. For a more comprehensive definition of persuasion, see Kathleen Reardon, *Persuasion in Practice* (Newbury Park, CA: Sage Publications, 1991). See also R. Dawson, *Secrets of Power Persuasion* (Englewood Cliffs, NJ: Prentice-Hall, 1992) for a layperson's guide to persuasion as a selling tool.
2. Reardon, 1–2.

Chapter 2.

1. See Reardon's chapter one in *Persuasion in Practice* for an excellent discussion of this issue.
2. Ibid., 9–12. Reardon describes this as a myth that "persuasion endures without effort." In chapter one, there is an excellent discussion on persuasion requiring an ongoing effort.
3. Ibid., 210.
4. Ibid., 5, 7.
5. R. B. Cialdini, "Interpersonal Influence: Being Ethical and Effective." In S. Oskamp and S. Spacapan, eds., *Interpersonal Processes: The Claremont Symposium on Applied Social Psychology* (Newbury Park: Sage Publications, 1987).
6. Ibid.
7. Reardon, 5–9 for a broader discussion of this issue.

Chapter 3.

1. L. Cooper, trans., *The Rhetoric of Aristotle* (Englewood Cliffs: Prentice-Hall, 1932), 8–9.
2. G. A. Hauser, *Introduction to Rhetorical Theory* (New York: Harper & Row 1986), 97.
3. Ibid., 97–99.
4. Ibid., 97–99.
5. Ibid., 99.
6. Story is from R. Dawson, *Secrets of Power Persuasion* (Englewood Cliffs, NJ: Prentice-Hall, 1992), 283–284.

7. See also D. Clark, "How a Woman's Passion and Persistence Made BOB," *Wall Street Journal,* 10 January 1995, B1.

8. Ibid.

9. Y. Aras, "A Lonely First Birthday for BOB," *Computer Retail Week,* 1 January 1996, and "Microsoft's BOB," *New York Times,* 14 April 1996.

Chapter 4.

1. L. Iacocca and W. Novak, *Iacocca: An Autobiography* (New York: Bantam Books, 1984), 208–212.

2. D. Kahneman and A. Tuersky, "Choices, Values, and Frames," *American Psychologist,* vol. 39, no. 4, 341–342.

3. F. Westley, "Vision Worlds: Strategic Vision as Social Interaction," *Advances in Strategic Management,* vol. 8, 271–305.

4. Ibid., 284.

5. Ibid., 286.

6. Reardon, Ibid., 11.

7. For more on value and belief amplification, see D. A. Snow, E. B. Rochford, S. K. Warden, and R. D. Benford's "Frame Alignment Processes, Micromobilization, and Movement Participation," *American Sociological Review,* August 1986, 51, 464–481.

8. C. W. Morris, *Signs, Language and Behavior* (New York: Prentice-Hall, 1949), 214.

9. A. R. Willner, *The Spellbinder.* (New Haven: Yale University Press, 1984).

10. E. D. Steele and W. C. Redding, "The American Value System: Premises for Persuasion," *Western Speech,* 26 (Winter, 1962), 83–91.

Chapter 5.

1. D. O'Keefe, *Persuasion, Theory and Research* (Newbury Park, CA: Sage Publications, 1990), 168–169.

2. Ibid., 160–161.

3. Ibid., 161–162.

4. Hauser.

5. For more information on the Myers-Briggs, refer to the following: I. Myers, *Introduction to Type* (Palo Alto, CA: Consulting Psychologists Press, 1987); S. Hirsch, and J. Kummerow, *Introduction to Type in Organizational Settings* (Palo Alto, CA: Consulting Psychologists Press, 1987).

6. P. Myers and K. Myers, *Myers-Briggs Report Form* (Palo Alto, CA: Consulting Psychologists Press).

7. Ibid.

8. H. Simon, *Administrative Behavior* (New York: The Free Press, 1976), 284.

9. R. Lindstrom, "The Art of Persuasion," *Presentation,* April, 22.

10. J. Carlzon, *Moments of Truth* (New York: Harper & Row, 1987).

11. G. Hauser, *Introduction to Rhetorical Theory* (New York: Harper & Row, 1986), 73–75.

12. G. Kelly, *A Theory of Personality* (New York: Norton, 1963).

13. Hauser.

14. Permission granted to reprint, J. Welch, "Speed, Simplicity, Self-Confidence: Keys to Leading in the 90's," General Electric Annual Meeting, Greenville, SC, 26 April 1989.

15. M. M. Osborn and D. Ehninger, "The Metaphor in Public Address," *Speech Monographs,* 29, 228.

16. E. Borgida and R. E. Nisbett, "The Differential Impact of Abstract versus Concrete Information on Decisions," *Journal of Applied Technology,* 7 (3) 1977, 258–271.

17. Gerry Spence, *How to Argue and Win Every Time* (New York: St. Martin's Press, 1995), 113.

18. Ibid., 115.

19. T. Peters, *Ten Vital Rules for Giving Incredible Speeches* (IL: Video Publishing House), 8.

20. Reprinted by permission from Steven Jobs.

21. I. B. Myers, *Introduction to Type* (Palo Alto, CA: Consulting Psychologists Press, 1993).

22. Ibid.

Chapter 6.

1. G. Hauser, 111–112.

2. This section originally appeared as a case study that I coauthored with Nancy Rothbard for the Harvard Business School. The case series is entitled Orit Gadiesh: Pride at Bain & Co. (A) (B), 1993, Publishing Division, Harvard Business School, Boston, MA 02163.

3. Nancy J. Perry, "A Consulting Firm Too Hot to Handle?" *Fortune,* 27 April 1987, 94. The 1991 data comes from *Consultant's News,* June 1992, 2.

4. The 1991 data comes from *Consultant's News,* June 1992, 2.

5. *Consultant's News* (Fitzwilliam, NH: Kennedy Publications), November 1992, 1.

6. Keith Hammonds, "Can Bain Consultants Get Bain & Co. Out of This Jam?" *Business Week,* 11 February 1991, 52.

7. Paul Hemp, "Did Greed Cripple Bain & Co.?" *Boston Globe,* 27 February 1991, 40.

8. D. Woodruff and K. Miller, "Chrysler Neon: Is this the Small Car Detroit Couldn't Build?" *Business Week*, 3 May 1994, 117.
9. D. O'Keefe, *Persuasion: Theory and Research*, (Newbury, CA: Sage Publications, 1990), 166.
10. Ibid, 166–167.
11. Permission granted to reprint, J. Welch, "Speed, Simplicity, Self-Confidence: Keys to Leading in the 90's," presented at the General Electric Annual Meeting of Share Owners, Greenville, SC, 26 April 1989.

Appendix 1
1. G. Morgan, *Images of Organizations* (Newbury Park, CA: Sage Publications, 1986), 23–24.
2. Ibid., 24.
3. Ibid., 24–25.
4. Ibid., 29–32. This entire section on Taylor.
5. In Europe (with exceptions like Scandinavia), Asia, Africa, and Latin America, the command style will persist longer, for cultural and historical reasons.
6. This text is taken from R. Suskind, and S. Alexander, "Fired Sunbeam Chief Harangued and Hazed Employees," *Wall Street Journal*, 14 January 1993, A1, A6.
7. N. Tichy, and R. Charan, "The CEO as Coach: An Interview with Allied Signal's Lawrence A. Bossidy, *Harvard Business Review*, March/April 1995, 72.

Appendix 2
1. T. Harris, "The Post-Capitalist Executive: An Interview with Peter Drucker," *Harvard Business Review*, May/June 1993, 115.
2. For more on the generations, see N. Howe and W. Strauss, "The New Generation Gap," *The Atlantic Monthly*, December 1992, 67–89, and C. Russell, *The Master Trend* (New York: Plenum Publishing, 1993).
3. Russell, 35–36.
4. Statistical Abstract of the United States, (Washington, DC, U.S. Department of Commerce, 1993), 152–5.
5. W. Kiechel, "The Workaholic Generation," *Fortune*, 10 April 1989, 50.
   6. A. Toffler, *Power Shift* (New York: Bantam Books, 1990).
7. J. Wilke, "Computer Links Erode Hierarchical Nature of Workplace Culture," *Wall Street Journal*, 9 December 1993, A7.
8. T. A. Stewart, "Managing in a Wired Company," *Fortune*, 11 July 1994, 50.

Index